CHARLES COUNTY COMMUNITY COL

P9-ASD-907

Energize Your Learning Environment

Some 25 percent of learning depends on the physical environment.

This is the first book to focus exclusively and comprehensively on the physical aspects of the learning situation for adults.

Written for:
• Presenters
• Meeting planners
• Teachers
• Program administrators
• Instructors of all kinds

Those involved in:
• Conferences
• Seminars
• Classes
• Courses

For experienced presenters:

Advanced, in-depth and current practical how-to techniques, strategies and tips to enhance your success.

For new presenters:

Comprehensive and concise treatment of all the important aspects of the physical learning environment and how it can help you improve your session.

Practical

More than 200 how-to ideas, tips and suggestions. Just one technique will help enhance your presentation and improve your participants' learning.

Innovative

Discover the breakthrough research on Presenter Space and a pioneering work on Learning Mediums.

Comprehensive

Covers all four key elements—the natural environment, the meeting room, learning mediums, and teaching tools.

Conceptual

This book will change the way you see your physical setting and its effect on your session.

Energizing the
Learning Environment

by William A. Draves

WITHDRAWN
SCCCC LIBRARY
4601 Mid Rivers Mall Driv
St. Peters, MO 63376

Copyright © 1995 by William A. Draves. All rights reserved. No portion of this book may be used or reproduced in any manner whatsoever without written permission from the author except in the case of brief quotations embodied in critical reviews and articles. Manufactured in the United States of America.

Published by the Learning Resources Network (LERN), 1550 Hayes Drive, Manhattan, Kansas 66502.

Library of Congress Cataloging in Publication Data

Draves, William A., 1949–

    Energizing The Learning Environment.

    Bibliography

    Includes index.

    1. Adult education.   2. Teaching.   I. Title.

LC

Library of Congress Catalog Card Number: 94-77347

ISBN: 0-914951-79-3

Printing

5   4   3   2   1

Dedication

For my mother, Alice Trist Thorkelson Draves,
who made our home
a place of learning as well as loving.

Other books by William A. Draves

How to Teach Adults, Learning Resources Network (LERN), Manhattan, KS, USA; First edition 1984; Second edition 1995.

The Free University: A Model for Lifelong Learning, Association Press, Chicago, 1980.

The Successful Presenter, Learning Resources Network (LERN), Manhattan, KS, USA; First edition 1988; Second edition 1994.

Acknowledgments

As a chronicler rather than creator of ideas, I first acknowledge those who are leading the field of adult learning. They include Malcolm Knowles, the father of adult education, whose work on self-directed learning and personal practice as a teacher is the model for adult learning in the 21st century; and Jerry Apps, whose advocacy of a more personal and interactive teaching style is the direction we must go in; and to Roger Hiemstra for his work in this area.

My appreciation also goes to Karen Powell at AT&T, from whom I garnered the phrase and concept of energizing the learning environment; to Su Bacon, my longtime editor, critic, and supporter; to my valuable assistant Mrs. Jo Wilson; to Janice Flanary and Carolyn Arand for typesetting and layout; and to my colleague and life's companion Julie Coates for her support and encouragement.

Finally, in recognition of the wonderful connectedness of generations and in indebtedness to my father and to my son, I acknowledge two other William A. Draveses who helped me accomplish this work.

My father, William A. Draves III, contributed the index to this book, as he has to my other works. My son, William A. Draves V, age 7, did the cover drawing. Their help has made this work a product of three generations.

TABLE OF CONTENTS

Part I
The Learning Environment

Chapter 1
The Apex of Learning

We have a long-standing fascination with the dunce cap, the symbol of ignorance, stupidity, and humiliation. It is a central feature of learning and our image of learning and how it takes place.

Even today, the dunce cap lives on in our collective memory as a sign of stupidity and humiliation. A few years back I wanted a dunce cap for my very own. So I researched the approximate measurements. I went to the local shoe repair shop, which also sold leather, and asked for white leather. A seamstress cut the leather, sewed it together, and then to modernize my dunce cap, sewed in Velcro attachments. When I travel I compress my dunce cap and pack it in a briefcase. And whenever I wear my dunce cap, audiences invariably get a curious look on their faces. They can't get past the dunce cap. It makes me look foolish in their eyes. It is not a mask or a costume—it has a much deeper effect. People really believe you are dumb if you put on that cap.

But the dunce cap has not always been a dunce cap. In fact, it originated as a sign of knowledge and authority. The dunce cap was worn in ancient times in Egypt and other lands only by the priests of knowledge, the advisers to the king who were responsible for keeping and expanding knowledge and learning. Only a few lucky chosen ones were allowed to wear the dunce cap, which we now will call the learning cap or apex.

In ancient civilizations the peoples believed that learning and knowledge came from the heavens, like all other blessed and welcomed acts. To help capture as much knowledge and learning from the heavens as possible, the learned ones would wear the apex. The apex would physically funnel the knowledge down and into one's head.

The apex was shaped in the form of a pyramid. And pyramids were believed to have scientific physical powers. Pyramids may or may not actually have different physical properties, but the literature documents cases to illustrate the argument. Animals have been found to be preserved in pyramids, for example. Thus the belief was not purely superstitious or mythical. In fact, the founders of the United States believed in pyramids, or at least wanted to hedge their bets. On one side of the one dollar bill note you can find a pyramid—just in case the ancients were right.

So the apex physically assisted in learning. It was a good luck charm and more. It was a helper, an aid in learning. It helped to funnel knowledge from the heavens into the wearer's head. It was a symbol of great esteem, accomplishment, and achievement. It was not a dunce cap.

Over the centuries the apex, as part of the traditions and practices of the ancient civilizations, came under attack and was discredited.

In the medieval ages, the apex was seen as a symbol of pagan religion and culture.

At one point in the 16th century two educational, philosophical and religious factions in the British Isles were opposed to each other over educational philosophy. Ironically, the dunce cap acquired its name from a famous educator.

Born around 1265, John Duns Scotus came from the village of Duns in Scotland. He became perhaps the greatest British medieval philosopher, defending traditional Scholastic doctrines against Thomistic innovations. He was a theologian and an educator.

In the 16th century the followers of Duns Scotus obstinately opposed a new kind of learning advocated by humanists and reformers. The opponents of the Scotists began to deride and ridicule the followers of Scotus by calling them "dunsmen" or "duns." And the duns cap, a symbol of the old ways, was then also assigned to the followers of Scotus and called a duns cap. Thereupon the apex changed from a symbol of scholarship and learning to the dunce cap, a symbol of stupidity and ignorance.

For the next several centuries the dunce cap was used once again as a real instrument in the learning process, only as a tool of punishment. That punishment, to sit in the corner, sometimes on a stool, and wear the dunce cap and be mocked by the rest of the students for one's ignorance, was supposed to be sufficient motivation to learn.

But when the apex became a dunce cap, something else happened as well. Society's concept of learning and how learning takes place also changed. Learning no longer came from the heavens. Now learning came from within one's own head, regardless of the physical conditions. It did not matter what the teaching methods were. It did not matter what the textbook was. In short, nothing mattered except the resolve of the learner. If the student did not learn, it was for lack of resolve. The "cure" or assistance for that, of course, was punishment. Physical punishment, mental punishment, emotional punishment: put on the dunce cap.

If the locus of responsibility was with the learner, then the external educational environment did not matter. It could be as constraining as possible. In fact, it was. The external environment did not consider the learner. It did not consider the individual.

So as the apex represented an age in which learning was seen as coming from the heavens, the dunce cap represented an age, still partly with us, in which learning was seen as coming solely from within one's own head.

Today our perception of learning is shifting once again. There are still vestiges of the educational belief system that holds the learner totally responsible for his or her learning, regardless of the external learning environment.

Because those vestiges of the learner as totally responsible remain, we continue to see the dunce cap as a sign of humiliation and ignorance.

Today, however, we are seeing our perception of learning shift once again. We are no longer seeing learning as totally originating in one's head.

We are beginning to see that the external environment does make a difference, sometimes a critical difference, to one's learning. A constraining environment can inhibit, curtail, or even eliminate one's capacity or will to learn. A wide open environment, a friendly environment, encourages exploration and discovery which leads to excellence in learning.

Learning, while it may not come directly down from the

heavens, is nevertheless enhanced and encouraged and stimulated by forces outside of one's own head. In fact, a United States Department of Education study found that the external learning environment can account for 25 percent of our learning. Thus, the origin, rationale, and utility of this book.

In *Energizing the Learning Environment,* we see that learning is influenced and enhanced by external factors. Learning is a delicate relationship and interaction between the learner and his or her environment. The biggest external factor in learning is, of course, a teacher, instructor, or presenter.

Although there is no substitute for good pedagogical practices, our presentation or class session can be greatly enhanced by a positive physical environment.

In this book we will explore the external environment, how it affects learning, and what practical techniques we can employ to enhance the learning environment. This is meant to be a guide for two groups of people. The first is teachers, instructors and presenters, those who interact with learners and conduct classes, courses, programs, workshops, sessions, or presentations at conferences and seminars. The second audience is administrators and managers of meetings, those responsible for working with instructors and presenters. Whether you are an instructor, teacher, presenter, or an administrator/meeting planner/programmer, you have an opportunity to change and enhance the quality of the learning taking place at your next program.

Energizing the Learning Environment is for those of us who give presentations and courses as part of what we do, either professionally or avocationally. We may do a session once a year or once a month, teach a course once a year or once a week. If you are a beginner or amateur presenter or teacher, you will find a complete overview and treatment of the physical learning environment and how it can help your presentation.

If you are an experienced teacher or presenter, there are several sections of original and innovative material, such as the concept and implications of "presenter space and participant space" and the notion and uses of "learning mediums."

By energizing the learning environment for your participants and learners, you can enhance and amplify their learning, their enjoyment, and their satisfaction with your program. This book will help you do that.

As we move into the 21st century, there are signs that the apex will no longer be seen as the dunce cap. My young son, when he sees the apex on my head as I wander around the house on weekends re-energizing my learning capabilities, does not look up at the apex and call it a dunce cap. He does not know what a dunce cap is. But he does know what the apex is. It is a wizard's cap and a wizard is a good person, a smart person, a knowledgeable person, a magical person. Once again the apex will follow us through history, reflecting our images and beliefs about learning. Once again, the apex will be a learning cap.

Chapter 2
Learning and Teaching in the 21st Century

The external environment can enhance and encourage learning, but it cannot create or force learning to occur.

Learning comes from within. It is born with us. Someone once said that learning is not a vessel, either half empty or half full. Learning is a fire. The flames can be fanned, the fire can be coaxed and fueled; and in some cases, tragically, the fire can be put out.

But the fire of learning comes from within. It is the choice of the learner.

Facts can be drilled into one's head. Behavior can be trained. But learning—that which encompasses the mind, the emotions, the attitude, and the behavior—that comes from the learner.

In the end, learning is a matter of choice. It is part of what makes us adults and human beings.

For centuries people have tried to create, instill, and mandate learning, without avail. The French essayist Montaigne once was asked how to motivate a boy to learn. Montaigne replied that if a boy refused to learn, "his tutor should strangle him, if there are no witnesses, or else he should be apprenticed to a pastry-cook in some good town."

Attempts have been made to legislate learning, force learning, and mandate learning. And those attempts may continue for awhile.

But the demands of societal well being in the 21st century are different from the requirements of the society of the 1900s.

Economic units—businesses, companies, factories, government, nonprofits, educational institutions—are being restructured to survive and prosper in the 21st century. For the past hundred years, businesses have been product oriented and operated with mass manufacturing principles. In terms of people, employees, that meant a narrow range of skills in understanding one's product and how one fit in with the efficiencies of mass manufacturing.

To prosper today, most businesses and economic organizations must be people or customer oriented, not product oriented. Many organizations are becoming more customized in their services and products, and customer service is a given. More and more organizations are in the service and information sectors. These economic units depend on employees with a broad range of skills in dealing with customers, information, problem solving, teamwork, and planning. In essence, most economic units need employees and people who are able to think, act independently within stated ranges, and be proactive. And the rewards for employees increasingly are measured not in time on the job (a good day's pay for a good day's work), but in results and measurable contributions to the organization.

All this means that simply "training" people will not work. Training has a specific behavioral outcome known before the training begins. Learning how to type, operate a machine, or fix a computer program involves training.

And "instructing" people will not work. Traditional pedagogical teaching with its emphasis on facts and transfer of knowledge from one receptacle (the instructor's notes) to another receptacle (the student's brain) is insufficient. Just instructing individuals provides no guarantee that behavior is learned or changed.

So instruction is inadequate because it does not create proactive learners or guarantee skill acquisition, only fact and figure acquisition.

We always will need training and instruction. Training aimed at skill or behavior acquisition and instruction aimed at information or knowledge acquisition are and will continue to be a part of the learning scene for all of us.

But the most effective learning, the learning that will make a difference for us will be voluntary learning and teaching, a sharing of ideas, knowledge, experience, expertise, and skills.

The goal of voluntary learning is to inspire individuals to be proactive, continual learners and teachers.

The joy of voluntary learning enhances our personal lives. You probably have experienced the elation of learning something new, of acquiring a new skill, of having a great debate or discussion, of seeing someone else grow and learn. Learning is a joy, a gift, and it is magic. Learning involves much more than our brains. It involves our heart and guts and body.

Learning is not a vessel to be filled, but a fire to be guarded, fed, and flamed. The techniques in this book are not meant to be gimmicks, tricks, ameliorative aids, or substitutes for voluntary learning. Some of them may be used in situations where participants are forced to be present. But they are not intended to lessen a bad situation. They are proven and effective ways of flaming the fire. Some of them are tinder to coax a little life out of the flame while others are kindling to encourage a roaring blaze. None of them are substitutes for a good teacher, instructor or presenter. None of them can force participants to be enthusiastic learners. All of them can enhance the learning environment so that committed teachers and willing learners will reap the most rewards possible from this wonderful and magical and mystical process called learning.

Chapter 3
The Physical
Learning Environment

Energizing the Learning Environment concentrates on the physical aspects of teaching and presenting in an educational session.

It is not intended to cover all aspects of teaching and presenting. It does not focus on presentation techniques, such as preparing notes or evaluating a session; nor on interaction techniques, ice-breakers, role playing, or group exercises.

This is so in part because other works have covered those subjects well. It is also in part because as the area of learning and teaching for adults grows, there is simply too much information on this expanding topic area for one book.

But few writers have explored the physical aspects of learning to any great extent. Here we focus exclusively on an area too often ignored or misunderstood, an area with enormous potential to enhance your session and improve your participants' learning—the physical learning environment.

The physical learning environment is composed of four elements:

1. The learning room, the human-built environment in which your session takes place;

2. Teaching tools, those physical objects that help convey your message;

3. The natural environment, such as the temperature and time of day;

4. Learning mediums, those physical objects that set the stage.

reduce barriers, act as stimulators, and assist your participants to learn.

We can chart the four elements in this way:

Position

	External	Internal
Human-built	The Learning Room	Teaching Tools
Natural	Natural Environment	Learning Mediums

Characteristics of the physical environment

Two characteristics of the physical environment differentiate and define the four elements. One characteristic is the location of the element, whether the element is external to the presenter and participant interaction, as are the learning room and the natural environment, or internal to the interaction, like teaching tools and learning mediums. The other characteristic is the nature of the element, whether it is human-built, as are the learning room and teaching tools, or is part of the natural world, as are the natural environment and learning mediums.

Our response as presenters and teachers to the physical environment needs to be a departure from most of our previous experience. Instead of passive acceptance and inaction with regard to the physical environment, we can change our response to the physical environment. We can move to actively engaging the physical environment.

We can adjust our teaching to accommodate it, as in the case of the natural environment; modify it as in the case of the room and room setup; improve it as in the case of our teaching tools; or most actively, create it, as in the case with learning mediums.

Modify	The Learning Room	Teaching Tools	Improve
Adjust to	Natural Environment	Learning Mediums	Create

Response to the physical environment

In the next four sections, we look at each of these components of the physical learning environment and how you can take advantage of them to enhance your teaching and presenting.

Part II
The Learning Room

Chapter 4
Re-creating the
Room Design

The room where your session meets may be called many things: a conference room, ballroom, boardroom, or even classroom, but never a learning room. Although your meeting room has been carefully designed and constructed, rarely is a room engineered to reflect how adults learn.

In this section we explore how to turn a meeting room into a learning room.

Most built environments are intended for purposes other than learning. Compounding the structural inadequacy of most meeting rooms are two problems of perhaps greater detriment to our participants' learning success. The first is that most of us as presenters do not understand the impact of the physical environment on our session's success, and the second is that most of us as presenters don't know what to do about it. Consequently, most meeting rooms are left untouched by the presenter or instructor, even down to the arrangement and location of the chairs. The fate of the physical environment of too many educational sessions is thus left in the hands of the building's custodial staff.

Only a few of us may have the chance to build a physical learning space for our sessions. Yet all of us can modify the existing physical space to enhance our participants' learning and their satisfaction with our performance.

You can modify your meeting room in many ways, and the building's custodial staff is often more than willing to help.

Before your session begins, you have an opportunity to improve upon its success by the way you modify the room arrangements.

Regardless of the condition and arrangement of the room when you enter it, regard it as a good start, not the finished product. In only a few minutes you can rearrange, move, post, remove, and change your meeting room to make it a benefit rather than an obstacle, to your session's success.

In this section we look at ways you can significantly modify or improve the physical space in which your session meets. In determining the kind of room you have, the way the room is set up, the comfort controls, the presenter space, and the way you manipulate both your presenter space and the participant space, you have many opportunities to enhance and make a learning environment happen.

Room Settings

Almost all classes and sessions take place in one of five room settings: hotel meeting room, traditional classroom, corporate board room, living room, or halls or multiple-use rooms.

All five settings have one thing in common—none of them were designed for adult learning.

The traditional classroom was designed for lectures. The corporate board room is intended for business meetings and giving instructions to subordinates. The hotel meeting room, the most neutral setting, has the fewest negatives or barriers to overcome. But it also has few positive learning features built into it.

The living room was created for conversation, relaxation, and hosting friends. And the hall or multiple-use space was designed for community activities involving large groups and large spaces, from potluck suppers and theatre to political speeches and voting booths, festivals, and fairs. None of them were designed for adult learning.

Consequently, you will want to modify whatever room you are in to turn it into a learning room.

Here are recommendations and suggestions for modifying and enlivening each room setting.

Traditional Classroom

The traditional classroom with its desks in a square facing the chalkboard is probably the most challenging room to energize into a learning environment.

The main task is to open the minds and elevate the expectations of the learners as they enter and function in the traditional classroom. The traditional classroom conjures up all the past experiences with formal schooling, whether that was 30 years ago or just last week. Either way, your participants will enter the traditional classroom with expectations based on past experience, and often that past experience has been pedagogic, dull, and formal.

A primary goal then would be to shake up the room to give participants the idea that they too should shed their assumptions based on prior experience in the traditional classroom and expect something new and something different.

Here are some of the things I would do to break up that traditional classroom.

1. Get rid of any podium.

2. Ignore the chalkboard. Bring in a flip chart and overhead projector.

3. Post a few signs around the room. Maybe get a computer banner printed and stretch that across the chalkboard.

4. Put a piece of candy or mint on the desk of each participant, along with a welcome letter, class outline, or interesting article.

5. Attempt to rearrange the desks in the room into a different configuration—any configuration, as long as it is different from the standard rows of desks.

Certainly during the first session I would break up into small groups by physically moving the desks into circles. This will not only facilitate discussion but also disrupt the physical arrangement.

6. Stand by the door and greet people. In that way, you don't give them the opportunity to resurrect old expectations and move into old habits.

This is also something not typically done in formal classroom situations. It will send a different and positive message to your participants that you are not going to act like a traditional formal teacher or presenter.

7. Play music beforehand.

8. Put a slide or overhead up on the screen 10 minutes before

19

the session starts and give people something to look at, or at least consider. The more involved and intriguing the slide or overhead the better.

9. Move the clock! If a clock is on the wall facing the participants, move the clock or take it down. The clock should be on the back wall where the participants can't see it.

10. Consider moving the participants around at the beginning of the session. Definitely don't let any seats up front go empty. Move people up front if desks or seats are left empty.

11. If the room is large, consider a Donahue-like interview with participants, going into the seating area and talking with people during the first session. This breaks down the unseen barrier between the presenting 'stage' and the audience seating.

The traditional classroom setting may be the hardest to energize. The traditional classroom is the least mobile and the least flexible of the common learning settings. Thus your task is to crash through the physical relationships and break down the pedagogic teacher-oriented climate that the traditional classroom is meant to establish. Do that by rearranging as much in the room as possible. Then as the instructor or presenter, move about the room and position yourself before and during the session in places where instructors and presenters are not normally expected to be. Stand by the door as people enter. Move into the seating area while you are talking to break down the space. Get rid of any podium at the front of the room. And be sure you don't fall into the traditional instructional behavior and attitudes that we have all experienced in formal schooling.

Corporate meeting room

The corporate meeting room is designed for meetings and serious business. As such, it is usually well-appointed, has comfortable chairs, and usually a table around which the participants sit. Sometimes there is great built-in audio-visual equipment.

The atmosphere of the corporate meeting room may well be genial. But this is where serious business takes place, where decisions are made, and people are supposed to perform for the boss.

In using the corporate meeting room for a learning room, you will want to use those helpful physical attributes of the meeting room. But you may also want to make the atmosphere less serious and more fun. In a serious business meeting, there are budgets, financial decisions, and the need to impress the boss. None of that pressure is helpful in the learning situation. Therefore lightening up the atmosphere may be helpful. For the best learning, your participants shouldn't have to worry about the boss, about performing, about even giving you the "right" answer. Smiles, a joke or two, and a non-evaluative atmosphere are more conducive to learning.

Here are the things I would try to do with the corporate meeting room to energize the learning environment.

12. Put up one or more signs. The signs would welcome people to the session or class. You might call the session or class something special, create an identity. How about "Welcome to Idea School" or "Idea Den" or "Socrates' Hangout" or "The Home of Mind Games."

Another sign might establish the relationship between the topic or content of your class or session and the mission of the company or organization. This would help participants see that indeed the class or session is important to the work place and is neither a frivolous break from the real action nor a needless and wasted diversion from getting back to making money.

13. Have some food or drink available. Make the food or drink different from what people might ordinarily have for a business meeting in the room.

14. Dress up like Captain Hook, Caesar Augustus, or Mary Todd Lincoln. Just kidding, sort of.

15. Put some fresh-cut flowers in the middle of the table.

16. Put a sheet of paper at each place welcoming people. Let them know this is a learning session and that the rules are slightly different.

17. If people are in the same organization, they may tend to sit in customary places. Put name placards around so people sit in different seats.

18. Begin with an exercise that gets people standing up and moving around the room.

19. Consider seating yourself at a location toward the middle of the table rather than at the head of the table. This will help create a more discussion-like climate.

20. If things in the room remind people of the business—this month's sales charts, for example, take them down. Remove things on the walls or in the room that are used in the business or are seen during regular business meetings. Put them away.

21. Consider using props and other items not normally seen in the corporate meeting room.

22. Don't let anyone leave the room to become involved in business, phone calls, or interruptions. Close the shades if the room has windows. Try to get the loudspeaker turned off for the room or that part of the building. Try to block off as much as possible the problems, worries, minor irritants of the day that await every participant once she or he leaves your learning room.

The physical environment of the corporate meeting room is usually pleasant and conducive to learning. What the corporate meeting room all too often conveys to the participants is an image inconsistent with learning. Often participants are drawn toward traditional roles, behaviors, and expectations, so that it is more difficult for them to make the mental leap from the current environment to your learning atmosphere. The corporate meeting room is where serious business takes place. Regardless of the premeeting jokes, participants are restricted in their roles, behavior, and attitudes. So your challenge is not so much the physical environment because that is normally comfortable and suitable. Instead it is remaking the corporate atmosphere into a lighter, more free-floating, creative, and unevaluative atmosphere where learning can better take place.

Hotel or Conference Center

Hotel or conference meeting rooms are the most image-neutral of all the common learning settings. Because they are so multipurpose in terms of types of activities held there, hotel meeting rooms do not carry the stigma or expectations that other single purpose meetings rooms, such as the traditional classroom or corporate meeting room, have.

Hotel meeting rooms are not without their limitations and challenges, of course. Hotel meeting rooms are often expensive. The meeting room charge itself is only one consideration. Food and drink can add considerably to the bill. And audio-visual equipment can range from reasonable to unreasonable, especially when we go beyond the flip chart and ask for video projection and screen.

If your learning activity, such as a conference, seminar or workshop, is in another city, then the issue of portability comes into play. Hauling television sets and computers and wall posters is more difficult if not impossible. And we find ourselves asking what we can take that fits into a suitcase.

Another limitation is the ability to control outside interference and physical conditions. If you are in charge of the program, you can take certain precautionary measures. If you are a presenter, you have less control. And in either case, there is still a good measure of luck involved.

Meetings, dances, and rock concerts can take place next to your session. Air conditioners can be loud. Room dimensions can be unworkable. And walls can seem to be made of cardboard.

Hotel meeting rooms also can have a sense of sterility to them. They can seem standardized, bland, unstimulating.

But hotel meeting rooms have a large number of positive aspects going for them. So many in fact that one could argue that of the five common learning sites, the hotel meeting room is one of the better facilities for constructing a learning environment.

Hotel meeting rooms are flexible, open to the addition or creation of a number of different environmental enhancements, and possibly most important, hotel rooms have minimal stereotypical images or prior negative experience for most participants.

So the task of creating a learning environment in a hotel is two-fold: 1) to minimize the potential for outside interference; and 2) to build a learning environment as stimulating and encouraging as possible.

Here are some of the things I would do to take precautionary measures and minimize risks.

23. When booking the room, ask for a hotel layout chart. You want a room that has the most solid walls and the fewest adjacent meetings.

24. Ask about the square footage of the room. Compare the square footage of your possible meeting room with the square footage of the last meeting room you were in. Is it enough?

25. Ask about how many people it will hold. Estimates will vary depending on how the room is set up. Theatre style accommodates the most people; next is classroom, then banquet and finally U-shape.

Whatever the estimate is for the kind of room setup you want, take 25 percent off that estimate to determine the real capacity. Hotel estimates of capacity do not take into account that your participants will want to breathe, have an aisle space, or might not want to have both shoulders touching other participants. So whatever the figure given to you, take 25 percent off that number and that is the real capacity for your group.

26. A hotel site visit is preferable. If you do one, try to peek in on another group meeting in the room you want, try to spend a few minutes without a hotel staff person to "case the joint," and if you have a colleague with you, try shouting through the walls to test the noise tolerance.

27. Whether you visit the hotel meeting room in advance or not, ask every possible question in the world of the hotel staff. Be sure to ask about construction. The hotel may be beautiful today, but the morning of your meeting they could bring in the jack hammers and tear the lobby and halls apart. Ask about other meetings scheduled at the same time. Ask if the other meetings require microphones or music.

Ask about the walls. If they are solid or air walls, you have good noise protection. If they are movable partitions and not air walls, you may have a problem, especially if there is a mike or music or a crowd next door.

28. Check out the room in advance. If the hotel is in another city, try to check out your meeting room the night before. This is when they set it up and you have the most ability to make changes.

At night the sales or banquet staff is usually gone; so work directly with the staff setting up the room. Ask them to set up the tables just the way you want them. Set the proper distance between where you as presenter or instructor will be and where your participants will be. Take into consideration meetings next door and lighting.

29. Tip the person who appears to be in charge of setting up the room in advance. This is helpful. This is worth $10. By tipping ahead of time you get the person working cheerfully for you all day. Hotel staff go the extra mile when you have given them something extra in advance.

30. Become good buddies with the person in charge of audio-visual equipment. Chat awhile, ask questions, be sure to get the person's extension number in case something goes wrong. Audio-visual difficulties are the number one killer of great sessions. Your audio-visual person can rescue you and spare you the perilous consequences of "technical difficulties" that otherwise might be fatal.

31. If you have not had a chance to prepare the room before your session, don't hesitate to try to rearrange things just before the start of your session, if you have enough time. Do this with a tip and big smile for the hotel staff. They won't like it. But your session's success may depend on your physical environment, and it will be worth it to your participants.

32. Check out the neighbors. Find out if there is a microphone involved. If you sense there might be a noise interference problem, introduce yourself to the other presenter and casually bring up the potential problem in a positive and supportive manner.

33. Check the lights, heat, and windows. Sit in the back of the room and see if you have a good view. For sure try the overhead projector or other audio-visual equipment to see if they work.

Now here are some of the things I would try to do to build a learning environment in the hotel meeting room.

34. Load it on. Do everything—flowers, music, mints, welcome sign, wall posters, morning news—anything and everything. The more the better. I have never experienced a learning situation in a hotel meeting room where there have been too many enhancements. They all go toward diminishing any sterility in the room and more important, toward building a different environment, a different world, one in which the participant can forget the rest of the day and the problems and be mentally free to explore and learn.

The living room

Living rooms in homes and sometimes living room-like arrangements in other buildings are common learning environments. For some kinds of learning, they are highly desirable and most effective.

The living room is, of course, suitable only for small groups, with a maximum of 15, and more comfortably from seven to 10 participants. It is not conducive to sessions or programs involving technical subjects or demonstrations.

Audio-visual presentations are awkward at best, and sometimes best left for another time and place. Flip charts fit in, and if there is even a little white wall space, slide projectors will be feasible. But overhead projectors may be difficult to use.

But if you are looking for discussion, ideas, creativity, feelings, honesty, problem-solving, or an informal presentation of information, the living room is an exciting learning environment.

The informality of the living room is its strength. There is a bias towards friendliness, casualness, a relaxed atmosphere, and non-hierarchical communication.

It does not have the problem of being too formal. There are few problems with role behavior and expectations that often accompany the other common learning settings.

It also seems worlds apart from the office or business world or whatever world one might want to escape.

The main task in energizing this learning environment is to adjust the living room and the physical environment to allow an informal and participatory learning environment to come through.

Here are some things I try to do with my living room to enhance it as a learning environment.

35. Reduce distractions. Determine whether you need to turn the phone volume down, disconnect an extension, have someone else answer the phone, or even unplug it for awhile.

If you have children or others in the house, lay down or negotiate some ground rules for activity, television, and kitchen raids. For some of us in different phases of life, a babysitter or money for a movie may be a good investment. Corral and confine pets.

If you have a daytime session, check out the sunlight and make sure that the sun will not be pouring in on some of your participants.

36. Rearrange the furniture for your session. Living room furniture is usually set for groups of five or fewer, not groups of five or more.

Push back the furniture. Open the circle more. You still want to have the furniture arranged in a circle so that everyone is facing everyone else, but you probably will need to push the furniture back and bring in more chairs to accomplish this.

Get chairs from other rooms, or borrow folding chairs if necessary. Put chairs in front of the television, cabinets, or even fireplace to enlarge the "seating capacity" for your group. A typical living room, not necessarily a large living room, can actually handle a larger group than we think.

37. If you have a flip chart and a tight fit in the room, put the flip chart in back of a couch or outside the circle of chairs. You won't use the flip chart for the whole session, and you can appoint the person sitting in front of it to be the recorder.

Place little occasional tables around the room for glasses and coffee cups, but consider removing a large coffee table if it is taking up too much space.

The result may not look like the cozy informal living room you are used to, but your participants won't notice anything. In fact, your cozy living room is probably too intimate for the number of people you have coming.

The objective is to create as round a circle as possible for discussion and visibility and to get as many people into the space comfortably as possible. It won't look like a scene from Better Homes and Gardens, but that is best.

38. By all means, have some food or drink. But not too much food. A dessert, a snack, and drinks are all fine. Coffee and soft drinks are helpful. Have the food or drink available as people arrive, or offer it during a break in the session. You don't want to disrupt the discussion with "Coffee's ready!"

39. As instructor or presenter, you should sit in a spot visible to everyone, but also one that allows you to take charge of the group.

Sunk deep in the corner of a couch may not give you eye contact and control of the group. Sit forward if you are on a couch. Move your chair just inches forward to create an edge of authority. Not enough to discourage discussion, but enough to gain control if things disintegrate into social conversation.

Be sure to have all your notes and necessary items there with you. Once you start the session, you do not want distractions or interruptions. You don't want them from anyone else in the house, and you don't want to create them yourself.

40. An agenda, written or given at the start of the session, will add form and shape to the group as a learning group, not a social group.

The living room is one of the more exciting learning environments because it allows you and your participants to share ideas, feelings, attitudes, values, and personal insights. It is one of the better formats for discussion, for hearing great thoughts from great people, for tapping into the minds of people who are less outgoing than others, for sharing information, for creating new ideas, for problem-solving.

Halls and multiple-use space

Halls and multiple-use rooms are everywhere. They are in churches, community centers, city halls and county courthouses, senior centers, social service agencies, libraries, hospitals, museums, and public buildings.

Multiple-use rooms are usually inexpensive. They are in buildings that are easily accessible and well-known to the general public.

Multiple-use rooms, however, often are furnished sparsely, almost to the point of being bare. And the number of added features and enhancements available from the building's owner is often minimal. More often than not, the rooms are much larger than what is needed for your class or session.

Thus, the task of creating a learning environment with a multiple-use room is to make the room size fit the size of your group, and then to build as many enhancements and features into the space as possible.

Here are some things I would do with a multiple-use room.

41. If the room has a linoleum floor covering, think seriously about moving your session or class to another room. Rooms without carpeting or at least floor rugs usually have awful acoustics and present hearing problems for your participants. They are also impersonal and sterile. A nice wood floor might be an exception, but linoleum, concrete, or stone floors present problems difficult to overcome.

42. Make the room fit the size of your group. If you expect a large number of people, or your event is a conference, this may not be a problem. Multiple-use rooms generally are well-suited for larger groups seated theater style.

But if you have a smaller group, say 30 or fewer, then many multiple-use rooms will be too large, and you will want to make adjustments.

One way to fill a larger room is to set it up classroom style instead of theater style. Your participants may not need tables in front of them, but that won't hinder their participation. The tables will take up much more room, so that you may be able to fill the room and not have a lot of empty space left over.

For smaller groups, find out if there are any partitions that can divide the room. Are there partitions in other rooms that could be moved? Are there bulletin boards that might serve as partitions? Can we hang a curtain on a wire strung from wall to wall? Is there living room furniture that could be used to psychologically wall off an area of the room and create a more intimate environment? Don't accept the space as is; work to create a subsection of the room that will allow your group to have a more personal meeting space. The effort will pay back in big dividends when the group starts meeting.

43. Set the room up the way you want it. Bring out more tables, or put some away. Make a U-shape if that works best for you. The staff running buildings with multiple-use rooms are often not meetings professionals, so they may always set the room up in the same configuration. Take the initiative to have it set up the way you want.

44. Think about bringing in items from the outside. Because multiple-use rooms are usually inexpensive, you could rent anything from chairs, tables, and tablecloths to coffee urns and theater scenery and have it brought in.

Just one or two outside items can make a big difference in the atmosphere in a multiple-use room.

45. Think seriously about having coffee and cookies available. That is one good way to personalize the multiple-use room and make it more participant-friendly. In many buildings the multiple-use room is near a kitchen or kitchenette. If not, find out if you can bring in a pot of coffee or sodas and snacks.

46. Tablecloths on the tables also will serve to make the atmosphere more comfortable.

47. If you need to try to fill the room, try setting up some extra tables and putting literature, examples, or other items on the tables.

48. When setting up the room, make sure you play to the back of the room. Don't allow people to sit so far back that they are out of your reach and involvement.

49. Put flowers at the head table.

50. To make things less formal, eliminate the podium and work off a table or overhead projector, or simply on your own. Or try getting a little table and putting it in front of you for your notes.

51. Put up a large banner on the wall.

52. Do as many of the other little extras recommended in this book as possible.

If you can size down the multiple-use room to the size of your group and can bring in items from the outside, the multiple-use room can achieve almost the same flexibility as the hotel meeting room.

Chapter 5
Choosing the Best Setup

One of the more critical decisions you will make for any session is how to set up the room. There are different ways to set up a room, each with different characteristics to it, each giving the participants a different sense of what is to happen and how they are to be involved. The right room setup can contribute greatly to creating the kind of situation and interaction you want in your class or session.

The room setup will determine:

a. Visibility and ability to hear,
b. The formality or informality of the session,
c. The level to which you want the participants to be involved in discussion,
d. The relationship between you as instructor or presenter and your participants, and
e. The group dynamics that will take place.

Room setup is one of the more critical ways you construct the kind of learning environment for your class or session.

The most common styles of room setup are these six:

1. Theater,
2. Classroom,
3. U-shape,
4. Conference or square,
5. Banquet,
6. Chairs in a circle.

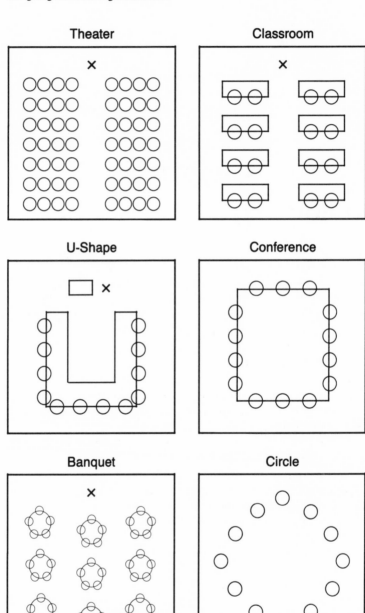

The most common room setups

They are listed in the order in which they are commonly used. But the frequency of use is not a measure of its usefulness or appropriateness.

In addition to the Big Six, Russell Robinson, a professor and respected adult educator, lists four other types of room arrangements. They are used less often, but offer variations on the other styles:

7. Herringbone,
8. Diamond,
9. Hexagon,
10. Chairs in small semicircles.

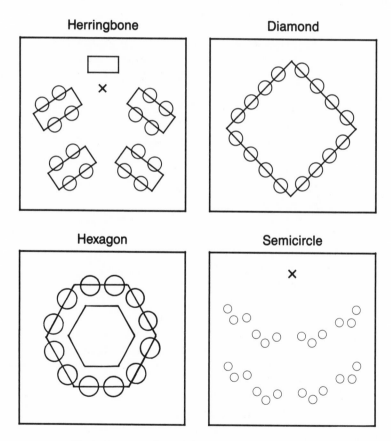

Variations on the most common room setups

While we will go into detail, along with suggestions and tips for improvement, on each room setup style, here is an overview of the Big Six.

Theater style
—Most commonly used
—Sometimes used when not appropriate
—Good for presentations and delivery of information
—Least conducive for discussion and group participation
—Good for large groups
—Has a presenter or speech-like atmosphere to it

Classroom style
—Takes up more room than theater style
—Good for note-taking
—Good for presentations and delivery of information
—Not conducive for discussion and group participation
—Has an academic or traditional classroom atmosphere to it

U-shape style
—Takes up more room than theater or classroom styles
—Good for groups of 10 to 30
—Combines ability to do presentations and ability to hold discussions
—Good for note-taking
—Has a business atmosphere to it

Conference or square style
—Good for small to medium sized groups from four to 20
—Good for discussion
—Good for note-taking
—Good for presentation
—Atmosphere is business-like

Banquet style
—Not commonly used, maybe underused
—Takes up more room than theater or classroom styles
—Good for medium to large groups of 20 people or more
—Suitable for note-taking, though not so suitable as U-shape and classroom
—Good for small group discussions and getting to know people within the larger group
—Has a business and somewhat classy atmosphere, especially with tablecloths on the tables

Chairs in a circle
—Best for creating informal and participatory groups
—Often sees presenter as group member, facilitator, and less of an authority figure than the other room arrangements
—Good for groups of four to 30
—Not good for note-taking
—Not especially good for presentations with notes or audio-visual aids

Continuums: Here is a summary of the Big Six room setup arrangements as they fit on a continuum for different criteria.

Formal-Informal
Most formal to least formal
Classroom
Theater
Conference
Banquet
U-shape
Circle

Authority Continuum
Where the presenter is seen as an authority figure
Classroom
Banquet
Theater
Conference
U-shape
Circle

Discussion
Most conducive for discussions and participant interaction to least conducive
Circle
U-shape
Conference
Banquet
Theater
Classroom

Accommodating size of group
From smallest group to largest size accommodated
Conference
Circle
U-shape
Classroom
Banquet
Theater

Here are considerations and tips for each of the Big Six room setups.

Theater style

53. Create an aisle. Sometimes a room is set up theater style without an aisle. As a presenter, you want an aisle. It allows you to come in closer contact with your participants. An aisle increases your range of forward-backward movement and makes it easier to talk with someone with a question.

A single aisle down the middle is best. This gives you easy forward motion from the speaker's area. Two aisles, one on the left and one on the right side, are less preferable. You may tend to play to the center section and pay less attention to those sections on the sides, and moving over to an aisle that isn't right in front of you takes more time and creates an unnecessary diversion during your session.

Difficult aisle setup

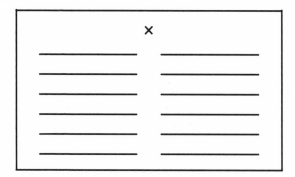

Best aisle setup

Also, if there are not walkways or aisles on either side of the seating, between the seating and the wall, it makes it more difficult for participants to come in. It shuts off a walkway for you as well. So if possible, you need to create aisles on either side of the seating.

54. Block off back rows. If you think you will have more chairs than people at your session, block off the back rows. Turn the chairs sideways and shove them together. This will give your participants the idea they are not to sit there.

Then if you miscalculated and more people show up than planned, they can and will unblock the chairs and sit in the back.

55. Turn the edges in. If the chairs are set up in a straight row, that often leaves out the people sitting at the ends of the row. And it is a more distant seating arrangement.

Take the chairs at the outer end of each row and turn them in slightly. You can either go for a more semicircle arrangement with the chairs, or a straight turned in arrangement similar to what herringbone looks like as a classroom style variation.

Either way, you've turned the participants to look more directly at you, and centered the attention on you. Either a slight curve or a slant of the chairs will focus the group on you.

56. Move the speaker area closer to the first row. Usually no one sits in the first two rows, and this creates distance from your participants.

So move the speaker's area slightly closer to the front row to lessen the distance. If you are used to speaking without notes, take a step up to the front row and speak from there.

57. Knock down the traditional speaker setup. As much as possible, try to rearrange the standard podium, microphone, and table setup.

This setup was designed to enhance authority and one-way communication. It creates distance, formality, and immediately confers expectations in your participants of a passive speech or lecture situation. Thus, it puts them into passive-reactive mode rather than expecting an involving, interactive session.

58. Do you really need to use the microphone? Microphones are commonly installed in rooms whether they are needed or not.

If you are in a room that does not require a microphone and you are not being taped, don't use a mike. It hampers movement, it can have technical difficulties, and it formalizes the session.

If you are in a room that really does require a microphone, find out if you can get a lavelier mike or a cordless mike. Either one will allow you freedom of movement and the ability to interact with your audience.

59. Get rid of the podium. Put the podium underneath the table. Move it to the back of the room. Get it out of sight as much as possible.

The podium is a physical barrier between you and your participants. It reduces interaction, discourages questions, and reinforces a "me-smart, you-stupid" physical relationship.

If you need to use a podium, jump up and down, wander away from it periodically, wave your arms, smile and laugh a lot, and try much harder to evoke questions and comments from your participants.

60. Move the table to the side. Generally, a table is set up at the front of the room in the middle. This forces you to stand either behind it, or come around in front of it. This limits your range of movement. It is assumed, of course, that you will stand behind the table, use the podium, and deliver a lecture.

The table should be there for your notes, handouts, visuals, and a glass of water.

Move the table either to the left or the right, off center in either case. This gives you a closer physical relationship with your participants and enhances your freedom of movement.

You can put your notes on the table next to you and refer to them as you need. You can move forward to your audience without having to go around a table. You can stand in front of your participants without a barrier.

The ideal situation would be to have a smaller table up front, half the size of a normal table. But this rarely happens. A longer table will do fine if you use only half of it to hold your notes, handouts, visuals, and water.

61. Move the flip chart closer. Usually the flip chart is placed about five steps or more away from where you are speaking.

Move that flip chart closer to you, so you can use it without taking extra time to get to it. A flip chart placed too far away from you is used less frequently, and flip charts are there to be used.

62. Put your first handouts on the seats. This saves you time during your session, plus it gives people a "welcome" sheet as they enter and sit down.

The theater style room setup has traditionally been used for speeches, lectures, and more formal one-way communication. To loosen that up, move yourself closer to your participants, encourage them to sit closer to the front, adjust the seating to center around you, and knock down as best you can the formal podium speaker setup.

Classroom style

Classroom style is an instructional mode, theater style with tables or desks added for note taking ease. Here are some things to think about in setting up a room classroom style.

63. Slant the tables inward slightly to center attention.

64. Give each person at the table enough room. A major feature of classroom style seating is to provide the space to be able to take notes and look at materials in an uncrowded manner.

A "crowded" classroom style setup does not make much sense because the same room can provide more space theater style. Because classroom style takes up more space, it should be done with a minimum of crowding.

65. Put tablecloths on the tables. Tablecloths soak up noise, are visually attractive, and more comfortable to the touch than tables without tablecloths.

66. Make sure there is an aisle down the middle of the room. This allows you to move closer to the participants sitting in the second row and back and interact with them.

Without that aisle, the participants toward the back of the

room will have visual and physical barriers between themselves and you. Those barriers are not helpful in maintaining interest and involvement.

Classroom style setup is a good instructional mode. But you will want to create as much incentive for involvement and participation as possible with this style. Slanting the tables inward slightly and creating an open aisle down the middle are two ways of enhancing participation and maintaining interest.

U-shape

The U-shape setup has interaction and participation built in. But there are some setups which reduce the effectiveness of the U-shape. Here are some things to look for.

67. The U-shape is intended to maximize discussion and presenter-participant interaction. But the more distance between people, the less interaction there will be. So measuring the proper amount of distance is important in setting up the U-shape.

68. Another important key is to fill the U-shape with your participants. This does not mean crowding them in, but a U-shape too large for your audience will diminish interaction greatly.

With the U-shape, you want to know ahead of time how many people will be attending. As people come into the room, you may want to make some adjustments.

A U-shape only half full can mean disaster for your discussion. In a theater style setup, classroom setup, or banquet setup, you can just move people to the front of the room. That doesn't work with U-shape.

69. The distance in the U-shape is controlled in two ways. One is the distance from one side of the U to the other side. The other is the distance between you as instructor or presenter and the back of the U.

You want to gauge both distances to maximize the room setup for discussion and interaction.

70. While the shape and size of the U often reflect the shape and size of the room, there are instances where you will need to modify the shape to maximize the room setup.

71. The distance from one side of the U to the other side should neither be too close nor too far apart. A distance of around 10 feet is normal for U-shape with 20 to 25 people.

If it is too narrow, people will be staring into each others' faces and will turn toward you and be less interactive. Also, you will find less space to maneuver when you walk into the U to enhance and encourage discussion and interaction.

On the other hand, if the distance from one side to another is too far, generating discussion "from across the way" is difficult. A distance of more than 20 feet would start to lessen the environment for discussion for groups of 20 to 25.

72. The distance between you and the back of the U is also something to gauge. For this you need to use your own judgment based on the size and shape of the room.

But if the people in the back of the U are going to be too distant, then it is worth it to widen the U and bring the back closer to you as presenter.

This situation can occur either in rooms that are long and narrow or in situations with more than 30 people.

73. If you have more than 30 people in the U, then you will have a Big U. You will have to have the sides more than 20 feet apart to bring participants at the back of the U close enough.

In some cases, you might want to switch to another room setup. Or you can just adjust to the Big U by working harder to create discussion and interaction.

Banquet style

Banquet style has some of the large capacity qualities of theater style, but with small group interaction possibilities. In setting up the room banquet style, consider these guidelines.

74. The back of the room. The folks in the back of the room are usually those with the most skepticism or the least interest. In a banquet style setup, if you put them together at a table they become a group.

One way of reducing this threat is to make sure all the tables closer to you are filled. You can encourage this by putting your handouts only on the tables up front and moving the water pitchers to tables closer to you. Those are usually sufficient hints that you want people to sit at tables closer to you.

75. Look at clustering or circling the tables around you rather than having them in a straight line across the room. The straight line of tables is going to put the tables at either end of the room at a much farther distance from you than the tables in the middle, and this will mean less interaction and involvement from those tables.

76. Just as the first two rows in the theater style setup rarely fill with participants, you may find the first row of tables also less popular. You may want to find ways to encourage people to sit in the front row.

77. Look at aisle space and moving space for you as presenter. What will be your paths of movement? Is there an aisle straight up the middle, or on either side, or a way for you to move toward the back of the room?

78. Put your speaker table and setup between two tables in the first row rather than head on with a table. This will lessen the distance between you and your participants. It gives you some space in front to move and makes visibility better for all the participants.

The banquet style setup is excellent for larger groups where you want to have some discussion and interaction.

Circle Seating

Circle style seating maximizes participation and discussion, with the teacher acting more as a facilitator and moderator than a presenter. Here are some tips for using circle seating.

79. Make sure participants are seated on both sides of you, so that you are part of the group, not facing the group.

80. To allow the group to control the discussion, push your chair back six inches and lean back. To gain control over the discussion, move your chair six inches forward, creating a slight bump in the circle, and lean forward.

81. If the session revolves around participants generating ideas, you can position a flip chart next to your chair for notes and to provide a record of the ideas generated.

82. If the session is a general discussion and no notes need to be taken, position the flip chart outside the circle in the back of your chair. In this way, if you have a visual point to make, you can rise and use the flip chart momentarily.

83. Use eye contact to keep everyone in the group involved. This is one of the more difficult seating arrangements for a participant to escape involvement with the group.

Circle style seating is not used often enough, perhaps because some presenters and teachers are needlessly defensive or threatened by its lack of hierarchy, its openness, its invitation to total participant involvement. Whatever the case, circle style seating should be used in more educational sessions.

Conference Style

Conference style seating is useful as a more formal setting for small groups. Here are some ideas for conference style seating.

84. Arranging the tables in a square, or as close to a square as possible, is preferable to a rectangular shape. The square includes more people and reduces any claims to hierarchy in seating.

85. For maximum discussion, seat yourself in the middle of a side, rather than at any end point or position that might be more formal.

86. Tablecloths will heighten the sense of importance of the session, plus be more comfortable. Tablecloths also can serve as 'modesty panels.' Coleman Lee Finkel, in *The Total Immersion Learning Environment,* makes the point that a 'modesty panel' or skirt that partially hides the view of one's legs creates an additional comfort zone for participants, especially women.

87. Name placards are most visible and useful in conference style seating.

Conference style seating allows participants to take notes and have other written materials in front of them. The table arrangement makes conference style more formal than circle seating, thus presentations are common. Participant discussions are welcome but usually not so free-wheeling as those taking place in circle seating.

Chapter 6
Moving In Presenter Space

Your room setup is not complete without determining where you as the presenter will stand in relation to your participants.

For rooms set up in theater, classroom, banquet or U-shaped style, you have some latitude in determining the distance between yourself and your participants.

That distance affects the degree of intimacy, warmth, closeness, and consequently, interaction between you and your participants.

Of critical consideration is the distance between the participants and the presenter.

If you are too far from your participants, your presentation will be more formal and the interaction less intense. If you are too close, your participants will feel uncomfortable.

As a rule, most presenters stand too far from their participants. The distance may seem comfortable to the presenter, but from the perspective of the audience the extra distance, maybe only a few feet, creates a more formal and less interactive session.

Many instructors and presenters measure the distance between themselves and the first row or the closest participant. What we really should be measuring is the distance between ourselves and the farthest participant.

The situation often is compounded by the fact that most people choose to sit in the back of the room, not up front. Thus chairs, tables, or seating in the front of the room often is left empty, making the distance between the instructor or presenter and the participants even greater.

Here are some tips on lessening the distance between you and your participants.

88. Draw an imaginary line across the room from the closest participant on your left to the closest participant on your right. You should be no more than three feet back of that line.

That is fairly close to the first participants. But it creates a more interactive and more personal distance with all your participants. The participants up front may feel a little close to you at first, but they will adjust.

More important, you will start to play to the back of the room, not the front row, and that is essential in communicating with all your participants.

89. Put the more comfortable chairs up front, thus rewarding people for sitting close to the front.

90. Remove the chairs in the back of the room, or fold them up, or put a rope or string across them, or turn the chairs inward to indicate people should not sit there.

That will move people up toward the front of the room. If you fill the available seating, you can always bring back those extra chairs.

91. Move toward your participants. If your participants insist on sitting in the back, take out the first couple of rows of chairs, or just move your setup forward to the second row so that you are closer to them.

92. When encouraged to move up to the front voluntarily about a third to a half of the participants will respond. It is always worth the try. Bribes, threats, and rewards have varying effects as well. The important thing is not to let the participants dictate the distance between you and them. If they do not help in lessening the distance, then you should take another approach.

What you are doing is creating an atmosphere in which optimal eye contact, interaction, discussion, involvement, participation, and feeling can take place. The "closer" to you they are physically, the closer to you they are emotionally and mentally.

Presenter zone

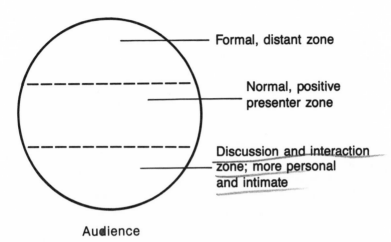

Formal, distant zone

Normal, positive presenter zone

Discussion and interaction zone; more personal and intimate

Audience

Another way to increase participant involvement is in selecting and filling the room. If you have a choice, select a room in which you and your participants will fill about 75 percent of the space, on average. If your guess is a little high, you still fill half the space. If you guess a little low, you fill the room. But it is far better to have a crowded room and people concerned about not enough space than to fill only 25 percent of the room. Complaints about the size of the room when you fill it are complaints of "success." Everyone will perceive that the session attendance is successful because you filled the room, no matter how small the room. You exceeded the expectations. And although everyone will be comfortable in the large hall with 10 people, failure will be the perception because the room is more than half empty. You could have a record crowd and if the room is more than half empty, it will be perceived as less than successful. And you could have the lowest attendance to your session or class ever, and if you fill the room, no matter how small, it will be perceived as a success. If your participants start off thinking the session or your class is a success, you have already built in the expectation that your class or session will be good, and with that expectation you start off with an eager and receptive group. Time and time again, given the choice, fill the small room and gain the perception of success, a closer intensity and greater personal interaction.

Another way we as instructors and presenters suggest a more or less formal atmosphere, and thus encourage or discourage participants from being more personally involved, is our physical stance in relation to a podium or table. Here are the most common stances in reference to a podium or table.

• Behind the podium or table. This is the most formal of presentations, and except for auditorium sized crowds, suggests distance from the participants, discourages active discussion, and is associated more with lectures and one way communication. It also may be associated with less experienced instructors or presenters whom the participants may perceive as needing notes.

• Next to a table, podium, or overhead projector. This stance allows you to be closer to your participants and yet at the same time be able to have notes easily accessible. By putting your notes on the overhead projector or table next to you, instead of in front of you, you gain more personal connection with your participants. Yet, you are able to refer from time to time to your notes or outline.

• Out front, no table, podium, or projector. Standing in front of your audience is the most inviting, personal, and interactive stance for a presenter. If you can carry it off without needing notes or outline, this stance often conveys the most authority and perception of knowledge on the subject at hand.

Sometimes you may want to create a distance between yourself and your participants. Yet, in general lessening the distance will create a more inviting and involving setting in which participants listen and participate more.

People Space

Because adult learning involves interacting with your participants, where you stand in relationship to your participants can increase participation or involvement.

For sessions in which you want to establish communication, interaction and involvement, you will want to position yourself so that your presenter space interacts with the participants' space.

Each one of us has a personal space, a little territory we subconsciously claim as our own. One person of British-American heritage standing in a room usually claims about two cubic yards of space. People of other cultures may claim more or less space.

As a presenter, you also claim a space at the front of the room for working and presenting. Your participants claim spaces for themselves in the audience, too, and collectively they claim Participants' Space.

The space we all claim is shaped like a circle around us. This claimed space is similar to the territorial space birds and wild animals claim for their habitat. The circle as the demarcation of our personal space extended in earlier human times to the group. Native Americans, for example, often lived in round homes such as wigwams and tepees; sat in a circle around the campfire; and used circles in their worship. Later white settlers would "circle the wagons" at night to claim their space and secure the camp.

As civilization gained dominance over nature in human affairs, buildings became rectangular rather than round, and today almost all buildings and rooms are rectangular.

But even as we build our meeting space rectangular, we still function in natural space which is circular.

Theater style, classroom style, U-shape, and conference style are all rectangular setups in rectangular rooms.

But superimposed over this rectangular setup are the invisible, yet always functioning, natural circles of Presenter Space and Participants' Space.

Understanding how presenter space and participant space operate can increase the effectiveness of your presentation and heighten involvement and interaction with your participants.

Presenter Space

Presenter Space is the circular space you use as presenter. It includes the space you use to show overheads, walk to the screen to illustrate and point, or go to the flip chart to write something. Your space also includes the table where you keep notes, handouts, and other items. Your Presenter Space is roughly 10 feet in diameter, or five feet from the center of your circle to the outer edges.

Here are two important considerations when setting up for your presentation.

93. Line up the center of your Presenter Space with the center of your audience. Usually you stand at or close to the center of your Presenter Space.

94. Set up the other equipment within about five feet of the center of your Presenter Space, or where you stand.

The optimal location of the screen is in back of you and centered, at the back edge of your Presenter Space.

Your flip chart should be off to one side, but no more than five feet away from the center of your Presenter Space. This will allow the flip chart to be far enough away so that you don't trip over it, but still be within your Presenter Space.

Accompanying this description is a diagram of a model Presenter Space.

Presenter Space Model

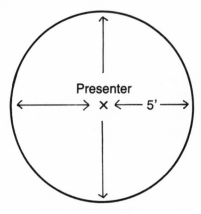

Distancing and barriers in Presenter Space

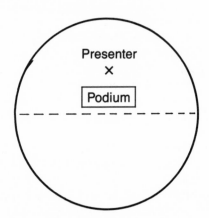

Presenter Space with equipment

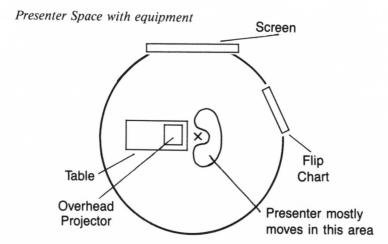

Knowing your Presenter Space has these implications.

95. Your inclination and energy level will mostly keep you within your Presenter Space. It requires conscious energy for you to move outside your Presenter Space. Staying within your Presenter Space allows you to move freely, easily, and without additional energy.

For example, if the flip chart is placed outside your Presenter Space, it will rarely be used. The next time you are a participant in a session, notice if the flip chart is more than five feet away from the presenter. If it is positioned too far away, the presenter rarely will use it and may even forget it is there.

Flip Chart improperly placed too far from the presenter:

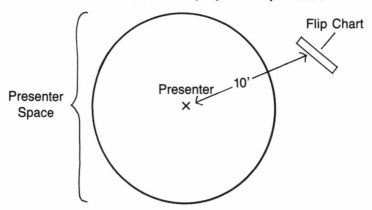

Thus, if the flip chart is set up more than approximately five feet from the speaker area for your session, move it closer to you.

96. Your participants expect you to stay within your Presenter Space, they experience dissonance when you move out of that space, and thus your movement distracts them and interrupts their learning.

For example, if a screen is set up outside your Presenter Space, it will be distracting to your participants if you move to the screen to make a point.

Screen setup outside Presenter Space

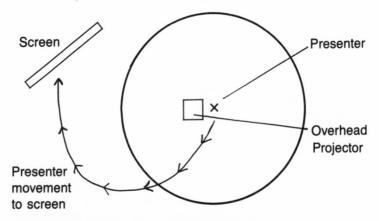

The movement from your Presenter Space to the screen distracts your participants.

The same is true for a slide projector, which normally must be set up in the middle or back of the room.

Slide projector setup outside Presenter Space

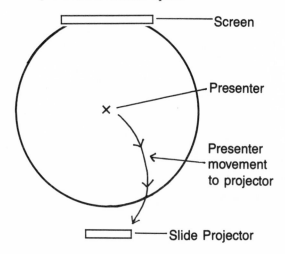

The solution for both situations is for you to stay within your Presenter Space. With the screen located outside of your Presenter Space, you can use a flashlight pointer to "work the screen."

In the case of the slide projector, use a remote control button or have a participant in the group change the slides for you.

In this way you are able to stay within your Presenter Space and maintain your participants' attention and concentration.

97. Presenter Space directs where you as the presenter can move. Presenter Space means you can and should move within your Presenter Space. You should not move outside of your Presenter Space, except to move into your Participants' Space, which we will discuss later.

You can move easily and effectively within your Presenter Space, and this enhances the learning. It creates motion, changes the visual scenery, and allows you to maximize the items, props, and audio-visual aids within your space. It also allows you to establish a more participating and interactive dialogue and communication with your participants.

SCCCC - Library
4601 Mid Rivers Mall Drive
St. Peters, MO 63376
WITHDRAWN

Examples of positive movements within Presenter Space

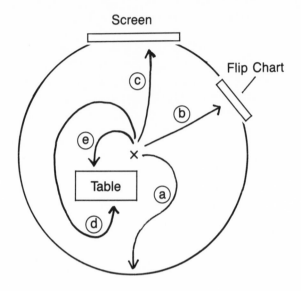

Here are examples of positive movements within your Presenter Space.

 a. To engage your participants
 b. To use the flip chart
 c. To point to the screen
 d. To sit on the edge of the table informally to make a point
 e. To get handouts, transparency, sip from a glass of water, to use an item on the table.

Moving around within your Presenter Space enhances your presentation and keeps the learning flowing, and your participants expect you to move around.

Your participants subconsciously understand Presenter Space. When you utilize your Presenter Space fully by moving around within it, your participants understand that you have control and feel comfortable with all of your Presenter Space. A presenter who moves freely and frequently around within the Presenter Space is perceived by the participants as being knowledgeable, an authority, comfortable with the subject matter and the group, and in complete control.

On the other hand, a presenter who is "chained" to one place is perceived to lack command of the subject matter or the group. The person may be thought to be uncomfortable or somewhat inexperienced.

So the perception of your knowledge and authority increases by your moving around within the Presenter Space. That higher respect, of course, increases your participants' learning.

98. Movement outside your Presenter Space, with the exception of movement into the Participants' Space, should be only for intended and deliberate distraction. As we noted earlier, when you move outside your Presenter Space, you distract your participants and disrupt their concentration and flow of thought.

For example, horizontal movement outside of your Presenter Space disrupts concentration.

Distracting movement

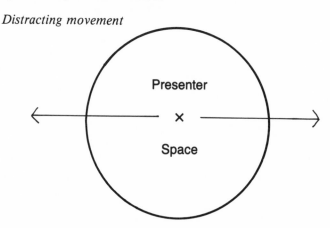

Whenever you see a presenter moving that way, you as a participant consciously are aware of it. That is not good movement.

The only time you should move out of your Presenter Space is to intentionally catch their attention, shock, or wake them up. But when you do, remember that their attention will be on your movement and actions, not on what you are saying. Move back into your Presenter Space if you want them to remember what you are saying.

99. Most participants respect your Presenter Space and will not invade it, even after your session is over.

If you have ever attended an all-day seminar given by a professional seminar company, you will have noticed that the company sells tapes or books or other items in the back of the room. This is often called in the seminar trade "back of the room sales."

A primary reason these items are sold in the back and not the front of the room, where presumably they would always be in view of the participants and thus sell more, is that they should be in the Participants' Space. In the front of the room those items would be in the Presenter's Space. Fewer people will intrude a Presenter's Space to buy. More will buy if the items are in the Participants' Space.

The coffee increases buyer traffic as well. The coffee, too, is put in Participants' Space in the back of the room where they are comfortable to roam.

The lesson is not just for selling items, but also for distributing them. If you have handouts or materials that you want most everyone to take, put them on a table in the back of the room or on aisle chairs near the back—anywhere in Participants' Space.

If, on the other hand, you have only a few copies and want only the most interested of your participants to take one, put them on the presenter's table in your Presenter's Space.

Participants' Space

Just as you as the presenter have a Presenter's Space, your participants collectively have a Participants' Space.

The natural Participants' Space, like that of the Presenter's Space, is also circular. This is the case even though the most common seating patterns—theater, classroom, and U-shaped—are all rectangular, and the meeting room is almost certainly rectangular.

Participant Space is a circle, not rectangle

Participant Space with seating

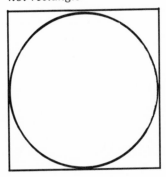
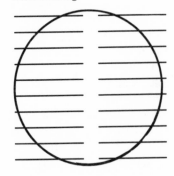

Two initial aspects of Participants' Space have implications for how you involve your audience.

First, some seats are set up outside the natural Participants' Space or are on the edge.

For theater and classroom style seating, these areas are in the back and on the sides. The far ends of the front row are also in this space, though not the middle of the front row.

These are your 'at risk' participants. Those who choose to sit in these areas often are more detached, circumspect, uninvolved, and occasionally disruptive participants. They tend to provide less satisfactory evaluations, and studies show they learn less.

You can try at least two approaches for these participants. One, you can encourage them to move to seats closer and more in the middle of the seating. This will almost certainly engage more of them and increase their interest and attention. And you can play to those seated on the sides and back rows, picking them out for involvement in exercises, examples and leading small groups. Be sure to respond to questions from people in these areas.

Locating participants outside Participants' Space builds an enormous barrier to learning and should not be underestimated. For one session, for example, participants meeting in a large room were divided into small groups for brainstorming. The group meeting at the far end of the room, outside of Participants' Space, came up with zany and irregular ideas. When the groups shifted positions, the new group gathered in the back of the room came up with unusual ideas. The off-the-wall ideas then were a function of the space, not the people.

A second characteristic of Participant Space is that the center of the space and the area middle and forward of the center will have the most energy.

Those most interested and those gaining the most from the session will be those seated in the middle and forward middle. It is not just that the most interested sit in this area, but that those who sit in this area will be the most interested.

When you are a presenter, your biggest supporters will be in this area and you can build the enthusiasm outward to the rest of the audience. Make sure people sit in this area before you start your session. For U-shaped seating, those at the four corners of the U will be the most likely to feel left out, and a gaze, question, or inclusive action will help include them. With the U-shape setup for

57

fewer than 30 people, the back side of the U will usually be within Participants' Space. This is one big advantage of U-shaped seating: it involves almost or all of the participants. If the U is set up for more than 30 people or set up with a long narrow U, however, then the back row may not feel so included in the session.

Intersecting Spaces

A final dynamic of Presenter Space and Participant Space is that the two spaces can and should intersect and overlap slightly. This physical intersection creates exciting possibilities for energizing the learning environment.

When the two spaces overlap slightly, you generate interaction, involvement, two-way communication and learner participation.

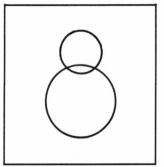

Presenter Space and Participant Space should intersect

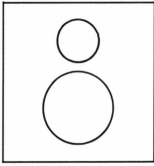

Spaces not intersecting

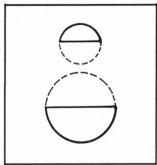

Speaking from the back of Presenter Space is more distant and formal; involvement with those seated in the back half of the room is difficult

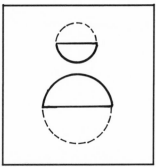

Speaking from the front of Presenter Space is more interactive.

When the spaces do not intersect, your presentation is more formal, distant, and far less participatory.

You achieve that involvement and participation in two ways. The first is to move and talk in the front half of your Presenter Space. When you speak from the center and back of your Presenter Space you establish too much distance between yourself and your participants.

In fact, if you are speaking from the back half of the Presenter Space, the distance between you and the participants in the back half of the room is so great that they might as well be watching you on television.

When you speak and move in the front half of your Presenter Space, you actively involve the front half of your audience and that catches on with the rest of the group.

Second, by spending some time at the intersection point of the two spaces you can gain greater involvement and participation.

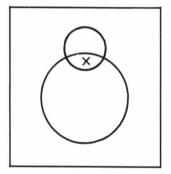

Position for interaction with participants

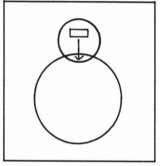

Moving forward into Participant Space is acceptable and positive movement

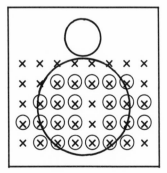

When participants do not fill the front rows you can move forward to intersect your Presenter Space with Participant Space and maximize interaction and discussion.

59

A common problem occurs when the presenter sets up so that the Presenter Space interacts with the Participant Space, but people don't fill the front rows. This pushes the Participants' Space back, and the two circles fail to intersect.

If you see people are not filling the front rows, you will need to move your Presenter Space forward to create that intersection.

Finally, you can create exciting, dynamic, stimulating, and interactive learning by moving from your Presenter Space into the Participants' Space.

When you do this, you invite participation, you challenge your audience, you risk, you dare, you generate the excitement of interactive learning with your learners.

The importance of invading your Participants' Space is that it enables you to create a dialogue or two-way communication. We call that two-way learning: the participants interacting with the presenter. Without that interaction, learning becomes a one-way communication and much of the learning opportunity and potential for the individual is lost.

So creating two-way participant interaction doubles or triples the learning opportunity or potential.

You create two-way participant interaction quite simply by welcoming it with your physical language—by intersecting your Presenter Space with their Participants' Space, and occasionally by invading or entering more directly their Participants' Space.

Part III
Teaching Tools

Chapter 7
Spicing Up
Teaching Tools

Teaching tools are those physical objects that enhance your teaching and improve your participants' learning. They are enormously powerful tools and we have generally scratched only the surface of their potential.

Few presenters and teachers use their teaching tools effectively. Most misunderstand and misuse them. Most people call teaching tools "audio-visual aids" or AV for short. AV is a limiting term. Here we will expand beyond audio-visual aids to include all physical aids in teaching. We also will view teaching tools in a new light.

Here are some of the more common and damaging misconceptions about audio-visual aids:

- The more AV the better;
- AV helps deliver information to participants;
- Major points should be summarized with AV aids;
- Low-technology AV aids are fairly simple to use and require little if any preparation.

The result is that in the majority of sessions, low-technology audio-visual aids are bland, black-and-white, wordy, and repetitive. They lack interest and add nothing to the presentation. At the other end of the scale, too many high-technology aids reinforce one-way communication and distance participants from learning rather than involve them.

Teaching tools supplement you as the presenter or teacher. They are not primarily for information delivery or one-way communication; they don't replace the presenter. They are not there to be repetitive either. They perform some tasks which help our presentation.

One reason we have teaching tools is that we as adults learn differently. Some of us learn best by hearing, others by seeing; some of us by example; and others of us by concept. Another reason teaching tools are powerful is they create variety and stimulate interest. And finally, teaching tools present your thoughts visually, in a way words cannot.

In the vast majority of cases, low-tech teaching tools are either more realistic or appropriate than high-technology tools. And with a number of significant advances in low-cost production of overhead transparencies, handouts, charts, and other aids, ample inexpensive and available resources exist for producing quality teaching tools.

A guiding principle underlying many teaching tools is that they are visual. The most important point about visuals is that you want to have a few good visuals rather than lots of them. One good visual can go a long way in making your presentation a memorable one. Lots of mediocre visuals, on the other hand, don't make a positive impression at all.

In "How to Conduct Training Seminars," Howard Munson advises, "If something can be adequately covered in the workbook or orally, don't have a slide on it. This argues against the use of visuals for titles, definitions or other subjects that can better be presented in the text."

Visuals are there to assist you in your teaching. They are not the whole show. You are the show, and they are enhancements and aids. If your session revolves around your visuals, you will be seen as the sideshow and your visuals will dominate. For almost all kinds of sessions, your visuals should play a secondary role to you as the presenter.

Think about this. If you were to lose your visuals, could you conduct the session? If the answer is no, then you may be relying too heavily on your visuals. If the answer is yes (but I wouldn't want to) then your visuals are playing their proper role—as enhancers to your presentation and teaching.

In this section we will provide you with a number of new and different tips and techniques for using visuals and other teaching tools.

Flip Chart

Flip charts are a simple but effective learning tool. They are easy to use and see, and they can help promote participant interaction. Flip charts are far more effective than chalkboards. If there is a chalkboard in the room, don't use it. Use a flip chart or dry erase board instead.

Dry erase boards are useful when you have a small group and no need to record the information. They are clean, and the markers come in many colors.

Flip charts excel over dry erase boards when you have a larger group and want to save the information. Flip charts have more versatility than dry erase boards. The best situation is to have access to both. Some easel stands hold both flip chart pads and dry erase boards, thus giving you a choice for a particular setting and session.

Here are some tips in using a flip chart.

100. Write "Welcome" on the flip chart before participants enter. Post a positive message immediately and welcome them to your session.

101. The best color markers are blue and black. Use red and green as highlighters only, especially if you have many participants in your session.

102. The best size markers are the jumbo, family size. They cost a little bit more, but the felt-tip edge is much broader and gives you a more visible mark.

103. Use flip charts as discussion starters. Discussion points are listed on the flip chart. When the page is full, it is taped to the wall with masking tape. This is still one of the better ways to visualize discussion points.

104. You can do charts, graphs, lists and drawings on your flip chart ahead of time instead of making transparencies for an overhead projector.

105. The flip chart is an excellent game board. You can play jeopardy as a nonthreatening test for participants using construction paper as a cover with the questions written on the flip chart.

106. Position the flip chart relatively close to you as presenter, with a slant toward the participants. If the flip chart is too far away, you tend to use it less often. It should be accessible for your spontaneous needs. Put it no more than five feet away from you. If it is too close to you, less than three feet away, you might accidentally bump into it.

Even though the flip chart is the most common visual aid in learning situations, its talents are underutilized. Spice up your flip chart with notes, colored markers, and pictures as well as spontaneous recording of key words or new insights.

Overheads

The overhead projector is still probably the top audio-visual device used today. It is low-cost, versatile, and easy to use. It requires little or no technical ability, and the overheads are easily seen by participants in all but the largest of audiences.

Next to the flip chart, it is probably the most used audio-visual device for educational meetings.

It is also probably the most misused device. The vast majority of instructors and presenters do not use anywhere near the potential of the overhead projector.

The most common and repeated mistake presenters and instructors make is that they put too many words on an overhead. Despite calls in just about every book on the topic to avoid this pitfall, presenters and instructors don't seem to get the message. It needlessly detracts from their session.

With too many words on an overhead, your audience starts reading rather than thinking about what you are saying. Many times half or more of the audience can't see the words, and they become frustrated. Some stand up and move forward. Invariably some request handouts made from overhead materials. This sometimes sends the presenter or an assistant to the nearest copy machine to make photocopies at an exorbitant price, or the presenter will use hours of clerical time back at the office the next day to make copies and mail them out to everyone. Then the participants receive the overworded overheads in the mail, and by then they probably have forgotten why they wanted them or have lost interest.

So why get on this treadmill in the first place? Instead, use some simple overhead transparency technology to produce readable, colorful, and visual overheads.

The key word to remember in doing overheads is "visual." You are creating a picture, not relaying hundreds of words. Your picture will assist in their learning. Your picture does not have to be complete, it is not a mural; you don't have to cram all the information onto one overhead. Instead, it is a snapshot, a frame in the movie. Don't try to make it more than that. It won't work.

For example, you have a form that is full of words. You want to talk about that form: how it should be filled out and what information is requested. Don't show the whole form on one overhead, making the words so small people can't see. Instead, make four or five overheads, each overhead enlarging a particular section of the form so that it is readable and coherent for your audience. Then they can concentrate on each section and understand what part of the form you are talking about.

You can be visual with your overhead even if you are using words or numbers. You can use lines, boxes, charts, graphs. You can draw arrows. You can make a word large, or in different type, or positioned in a certain way so that it creates a visual relationship to the other word. You can do many things without even using a picture, clip art, or other more commonly used techniques.

Using a few exciting tactics, you can turn dull overheads into visual learning aids. Here are some ideas.

107. Colorburst blue background. You will get oohs and ahhs from your participants when you use a Colorburst overhead.

The overhead background is blue, itself a relief to the eyes. Then the participants become excited when you write on the blue background and the letters come out yellow, or red, or green, or orange.

The effect is a visual delight.

Somehow the special marking pens—yellow, red, green or orange—mark through, destroy, or evaporate the blue background on the overhead, and you get words or drawings in the color of your marking pen.

The blue transparencies can be used only once, and then you have to discard them. So they do cost more than clear transparencies that can be washed and reused. The marking pens are special to the Colorburst transparency—a regular overhead marker will not work.

This is an innovative and remarkable improvement in overhead transparencies.

The Colorburst blue transparencies are available from stationery stores. Keep trying office supply and stationery stores until you find one that can order them for you. The transparencies usually come with a marker or two, and you can order extra markers separately.

108. Colorburst plus. Here's another way to use the Colorburst blue transparencies for a breakthrough visual sensation.

If you have a clear transparency with words or a chart on it, put a Colorburst blue transparency on top of it. Your audience then will see the pre-printed transparency, only with your black ink on a blue background instead of a white background. That in and of itself is much easier on the eyes, and a big improvement.

But wait. There's another trick you can use. Then you can take your Colorburst marker and "erase" the blue over a word or number about which you are talking. The "erased" part now is yellow, red, or whatever your marker is, and you can see your pre-printed black words through yellow, thus distinguishing it from the rest of your overhead. You can take this a long way, marking through words, highlighting the "good" words in yellow, the "bad" words in red, the four-step process in green, or whatever.

After you are done, throw away the Colorburst blue transparency, keep your pre-printed one on the clear transparency, and you can do it all over again at your next session or presentation.

109. Color transparencies. If you have pre-printed or made up transparencies, you no longer need to use the clear transparencies for glaring white background.

Red, blue, green, and yellow transparencies are now available, and you can use a copy machine to put your overheads on a color background. Order them from an office supply or stationery store.

110. Four-color transparencies. Copy centers now have four-color copiers, so you can take photographs, pictures from magazines, drawings, or any other multi-color picture and get a transparency in full color.

The four-color copiers do not always have the same clarity as the original photographs, but they still provide a visual step up for the overhead world.

111. Desktop. Use desktop publishing to create different fonts and typestyles, clip art, larger or smaller letters, graphs, boxes, and charts. The more professional the production, the better the overhead is absorbed by your participants.

112. Overhead notebooks. If you have a number of overheads, you can put them in clear see-through envelopes that fit in a three-ring binder. You can write notes to yourself on the sides of the envelopes to describe the overhead.

The envelopes protect your overheads, keep them in order, and provide a ready reference for you. Instead of sorting through all your overheads every time you present, you just grab your notebook and you are off and running.

Although the overhead projector itself has not changed much in the last decade or so, the materials you can use with the overhead have greatly improved, making the overhead transparency a low cost, easy to use, yet effective medium for enhancing your presentation. Don't forget—make it visual, not wordy. Your participants will appreciate it.

Chapter 8
Stirring
Imaginations Visually

Handouts

Handouts are often an afterthought. They often repeat the comments or even the entire text of the presentation. Too often handouts do not add to the content presented in the session.

Yet handouts can be an immensely useful tool for you and your participants.

Here are some suggestions for using handouts productively.

113. Use not just colored stock for your handouts, but Astrobright colors. These stock colors burst onto the scene and are downright beautiful. Your handouts will pop out and be distinctive if you use Astrobright colors. Put the pastels away; go for the bright colors.

Here's my ranking of the best colors for handouts.

• Astrobright yellow. My all time favorite. Good for lots of copy, stands out.

• Ivory. A little classier.

• Astrobright light green.

• Astrobright dark blue. Good for sparse copy or charts.

• Astrobright orange. Good for lots of copy.

• Astrobright red. Good for sparse copy or charts.

• Tan.

• Canary yellow.

White is so overused I try to stay away from it, except for handouts which have lots of pages of the same content or item, such as a five-page statistical report.

114. For handouts with lots of copy, use the lighter colors, such as yellow, ivory, light green, orange.

For handouts with only a few words or graphs and charts, you can use the dark colors like blue, purple, dark red, and dark green. Mix up the colors of the stock. Don't use one colored stock for all your handouts, use a different color for each handout.

115. Don't pass out your handouts all at once. Each time you give something to your participants, they think of it as a bonus. So if you give out all four handouts all at once, then you have given your participants one set of handouts. But if you give them out individually during your presentation, each handout will be appropriately linked to an item or content area and you will increase the number of gifts to your participants.

116. For short sessions with many participants, recruit others to distribute your handouts. Every minute you spend distributing handouts is time away from the session, and a setback for the rhythm, pace, and enthusiasm of the session.

In large groups have a few participants distribute handouts for you while you continue with your presentation. When you are talking while they are distributing, try to elaborate on a previous point or make a side comment. Don't try to address a handout that the back of the room doesn't have yet.

117. Look for handouts one page in length, maybe the back side also. Shorter handouts are read more, valued more.

118. If you have several handouts, put the first one on the participants' tables or chairs as they enter the room. This gets them started, makes them feel as though you are prepared, and sets the direction for the course of the session.

119. Generally, figure out the price of paper and cost of copying. If that is too much of a hassle, then a few pennies won't matter to you. The guideline is that too many handouts are better than too few. Few people complain about too many handouts. They may not read them, but they are seen as a bonus or a plus rather than a minus.

120. If you are using overheads and you know people will want the information on the overheads, put that information into handouts beforehand. People will ask for copies of the overheads if the information is useful to them or if so much information is on the overhead that they cannot simply copy a few words. If you have "information" overheads, make them available as handouts as well.

Charts and Graphs

Charts and graphs are the language of business, for good reason. Recently I was sitting on an airplane next to an insurance executive on his way to make a presentation before the corporation that owns the insurance company. None of the people at the corporation understand insurance, he noted. And when I saw his presentation notes, they were almost all charts and graphs.

Charts and graphs visually explain concepts, ideas and information in a way that is more understandable. That is especially the case for people not familiar with the subject or topic at hand.

For a great many situations, charts and graphs can make your point more clearly and understandably than words.

Here are some tips in using charts and graphs.

121. Make sure the numbers add up. One of the more common mistakes is that the numbers in the chart don't add up to the total. The percentages may not add up to 100 percent, for example.

122. Make sure the explanation is crystal clear. The caption has to explain what the numbers are, and for what universe they are valid. Don't leave your participants guessing as to whether the number 1234 is for one year, two years, all years, or whatever.

123. Keep it simple. The essence of charts and graphs is to make numbers and words understandable through simplicity and visualization. Too many numbers and words make charts hard to understand. Instead, make two or three charts. Three simple charts are much easier to understand than one complex one.

124. Use the proper graph or chart. Use a pie chart when all the slices of the pie add up to 100 percent. Use line charts when the chart illustrates something over time. Use bar graphs when comparing one bar to another bar on the graph. Making a poor choice in which type of graph or chart to use can confuse the reader.

Graphs and charts are physical, visual aids that turn complex ideas into understandable concepts.

Props

Props are helpful but underutilized learning tools. They are relevant to most any session or class. They provide variety, give people something to play with mentally, and visually summarize your message.

Some props are related at first glance to your subject or topic area. If you are explaining about a particular kind of wrench, it helps to have that wrench available and hold it up.

But another and more extensive use of props is to summarize your message. On first glance, these props have nothing to do with your subject matter. It is only on explanation that the props become relevant to your subject or topic.

Here are some tips on using props.

125. Almost anything can be a prop. A good prop is a recognizable but unusual item. For example, for a prop to "shed light on the subject" a lamp would not be an interesting prop; a lantern would be a better one, as might be a play stick of dynamite or fireworks candle.

126. Some of the better props are playful. A good source for playful props are toys. If you have young children at home, you have a ready source. Toys bring out a sense of wonderment even in adults and are associated with creativity in the first place.

If you don't have a lot of toys around the house, head to the toy store. Aisles of inexpensive props are just waiting for you.

Some of the toys I've found to be good props include a toy rocket ship, a glove with monster fingernails for scratching, and a toy battery-operated turtle.

127. Use props to illustrate your three to five most important points. Your props can illustrate points at the beginning of the presentation, or they can be used at the end to summarize your most important points. Either way, the visualization of the three to five points will help your participants remember them as well as maintain their undivided attention. If you've got more than seven points, try something other than props. Props are good for as many as seven points. After that too many props are hard to remember, and they lose effect.

128. Put your props into a "Magic Kit." You can illustrate your subject or topic with a "Magic Kit." I have used the magic kit to illustrate everything from "Magic Teaching Kit" to the "Magic Finance Kit."

Tape colored paper all around a regular cardboard box, and write "Magic _____ Kit" on it. Pull the props out one at a time to illustrate your main points.

129. Bring one prop for each class. An excellent teaching technique is to bring one prop for each class meeting, and let the prop become the theme. The prop represents the topic of the class for that session.

130. Do a magic trick or two. Some magician's props are appropriate and fun to use. Work the magic into your regular presentation. Don't say, "Now I'm going to do a magic trick." Instead, just do it as part of your talk or explanation. It will get people wondering and watching to see if you do another magic trick.

For example, one effective presenter had a book whose pages gave the impression that they changed instantly. The first time he riffled through the pages, the pages were blank. The second time they had black-and-white drawings. And the third time he riffled through the same pages of the book the drawings were colored in. A simple but effective teaching device.

131. Pick props that don't break, are not valuable, and pack or ship well.

Props add variety to your presentation or instruction. They also aid in visualizing your spoken or written points or message. And they are fun for the participants. They are not used enough by instructors and presenters. Props give you an opportunity to make a playful visual impression that is not only good presentation, but also good learning.

Chapter 9
Adding A Touch
Of High Tech

High Tech

We are entering a period of high-technology innovation in society. Laser lights, holograms, CD-ROM, interactive media, and many other new technologies will continue to amaze us for several years to come.

A number of high technology teaching tools may well add immeasurably to our learning environments. But many others will either not be appropriate or simply be infeasible for most educational sessions.

Many high-technology aids have one of two problems.

• Many high-technology aids are so expensive they are practical only for corporate use and built-in training centers. Even when such equipment is available for rental, the costs for a single usage are too high for most presenters and situations. Along with the high cost often is associated difficulty or fragility in packing, travel and setup; so that portability is also either inconvenient, expensive, or both.

• Many high-technology products are developed not so much as aids for a personal, interactive participant-presenter dialogue, but as alternative means of transferring information.

As such, these high-technology products may be effective for lecture or one-way communication sessions. But they don't fit into a session built on presenter-participant interaction. Technology products that project onto a screen for a period of time, require a darkened room, or lack interaction of presenter and participants tend to inhibit involvement and discourage participant-centered learning.

That said, here is a brief summary of some helpful high tech products at this time.

LCD units: LCD, or liquid crystal display, units are placed on an overhead projector and then connected to a computer, allowing the presenter to display whatever is on the computer screen onto the wall screen so everyone can see it. It is a tool whose usefulness began with, but extends beyond, software demonstrations or presentations.

Electronic overhead projector. This newly developed overhead projector needs no transparencies. It works more like a video camera so that any physical object can be placed on it and displayed on the screen. This eliminates the need to prepare transparencies. It also allows materials spontaneously contributed by participants to be shown as overheads. It projects in color and even has a "zoom" lens that can do close-up projections.

For more on the latest high tech audio-visual products, we recommend two periodicals, *Presentation Products* and *Technological Horizons in Education.*

Video

Video is a powerful teaching tool if used as a supplement to your presentation. Here are some thoughts on strengthening video segments.

132. The most stimulating uses of video are as short segments to illustrate your presentation. Severely time-edit your video segment to no more than 10 percent of your total time. A short good segment is far better than a long one. Most television news stories are two to three minutes long, for example.

133. Video is a better audio mode than an audio-tape player. With audio tapes, participants have nowhere to look, creating an awkward situation. Video provides an acceptable audio mode.

134. Try not to darken the room too much because it makes the video segment more a one-way 'show' than an illustration.

135. Spend as little valuable session time as possible starting the video segment. Have it lined up at the start of your excerpt beforehand, or dub the segment onto a blank tape to avoid confusion. Don't spend session time rewinding the tape.

Video, if used sparingly and as an interjection or illustration, holds your participants' attention and makes a visual point. When a video segment runs on too long, you risk making your session a TV show, a one-way communication: one that may inhibit rather than encourage discussion. So keep your video segment in proportion to the overall length of your total session time together.

Slides

Slides can provide visually exciting, dynamic, and crisp colorful images to complement your presentation if used appropriately. Here are some ideas about using slides.

136. If the visual, for example, a chart or graph or even picture, can be almost as effectively shown with an overhead, use the overhead.

137. Use only a handful of slides as an illustration of your points or visual enhancement. Avoid a slide show.

138. Use a series of slides as an exciting session opener or as a closer. The first use piques interest, the latter is a colorful closer.

Slide projection has these drawbacks and limitations.

• Darkened room. The biggest drawback is that showing slides places participants in a darkened room. Participants sitting in the dark cannot take notes, cannot see you well, and can lose interest, or even fall asleep.

• Production costs. Costs for producing slides, especially graphs and charts, are higher and involve more lead time than other visual techniques.

• Projector location. Unlike an overhead projector which stands next to the presenter and actually can be an interactive device, the slide projector usually is located in the back of the room or in the middle of your participants. The projector is more difficult to control and operate.

• The proverbial slide show. Participants often see slides as a slide show, an extended slide tour, rather than as an illustration or visual. Slide shows are long, sometimes boring, and too much 'show and tell.'

If your visual is best conveyed with slides, use slide projection. But use slide projection judiciously to maximize its positive qualities.

Part IV
The Natural Environment

Chapter 10
Reacting To
Time of Day

Although most learning situations take place indoors in human-built buildings, we cannot escape our natural environment and its effect on our learning and teaching.

The natural environment includes the sun, moon, and our internal body rhythms.

Instead of ignoring or trying to change the natural environment, the easiest and most effective path is to adjust our teaching behavior to the natural environment. That may mean a small group exercise after lunch instead of a lecture, or holding your session in the fall instead of the spring to gain not only greater attendance but also more attention from your participants.

In this section we look at the natural phenomena affecting your session and then discuss some strategies.

Time of Day

The time of day is a physical phenomenon that affects your participants. Our physical energy rises and declines during the day and evening. Each time frame can be productive by mixing different teaching and presentation techniques to heighten the participants' learning.

Here is a comparative look at the time frames, along with suggestions for the kind of teaching and presentation techniques that most enhance learning.

8 to 10 a.m. Early morning time frame

This is a wake-up time for most people. Your participants' physical and cognitive energy may need to be brought out.

139. "Wake-up" exercises are definitely helpful. These can include simply having participants state their name and where they are from and possibly their interest in the subject at hand. Some physical movement helps get the blood flowing during the early morning. Having people stand when they introduce themselves is a subtle technique to achieve this.

140. If this is the first session of the day or the first class, your participants may come with some expectations, interests, or even problems and concerns. Letting them vent their thoughts a little bit during the first meeting or first time frame often gets them involved. Because they have had a chance to comment, they are generally more accepting of what you say as instructor or presenter.

141. Writing a list of questions on the flip chart or overhead at this time of day is another way to "wake up" your participants and involve them more quickly. Sometimes that first one or two questions may take awhile. Allow some silence or encourage questions with a present.

142. If you are teaching or presenting throughout the day, the early morning is best suited for introduction, overview, and other information that is content-specific but not the most demanding cognitively from your participants.

If the early morning is the only time of the day for your class or session and you have cognitively demanding material, then you might want to spend a little more time in interactive exercises, discussion, physical movement, and other participant involvement time to make sure all the mental chutes are open and ready for your message. It also might help to allow five to 10 minutes as an overview or introduction to the subject before you delve into the demanding content.

143. You also may find that participants need some course content before they can be involved in a group discussion or provide reaction and feedback to your comments.

144. It may help your presenting or teaching skills to err slightly on the dramatic, to be more movement-oriented and energetic during the early morning.

10 a.m.-noon. Late morning time frame

For most participants, this is a peak learning time. It is when their physical and mental energies are highest. They are most receptive to and able to absorb new ideas and techniques. If your session or class is scheduled during the late morning, you are blessed.

In this time frame, you have an opportunity to deliver the most content. If you are teaching or presenting throughout the day, the late morning is optimal for new content, information, new ideas, and techniques.

145. Blast away. Give it your best shot. Deliver your content in as much detail and sophistication as is necessary or possible because this is the time of day when your participants are apt to retain the most information.

You can do discussions and interactive exercises, but if you have limited time for content, this is the best time of the day for that. Don't sacrifice your content during this time format.

For American audiences, be sure to end your session around noon. Your participants will start fading just before, at or just after noon. You can drag them along for 10 minutes or so, but not beyond that. It is best to break when participants have felt satisfied and had enough, not beyond that time.

1 to 2 p.m. Early afternoon time frame.

After lunch your body uses energy to digest food, and the energy is sapped from your brain. Many participants feel a little tired and a little lazy.

Straightforward content presentation is extremely difficult during this time frame. That's why "after-dinner" speakers are usually light-hearted and humorous—the heavy content is not so well-received after a meal.

146. A good remedy for the early afternoon let-down time is to involve your participants in discussions or other exercises. If they have to talk and be involved with others, they will stay awake and re-energize.

After your group discussions or break-outs, they will be more alert and then ready for your content.

147. If you are not able to spend time in discussions or group activities, sprinkle your presentation with little energizing activities. One presenter always has a line something like, "This next point is so important I want you to stand while I say it." The

85

point made while everyone is standing will be remembered better, and the standing also serves to get people to move and stretch without losing control of the group.

148. You also can have small discussion times, such as having participants spend two minutes talking with the person next to them, and then bringing the group back together.

In the early afternoon, the more participant interaction and involvement, the better.

2 to 3:30 p.m. Mid-afternoon time frame.

The mid-afternoon time frame is when both content and discussion are well-received, though not quite so well as the late morning time frame. But physical energy is at a reasonable level and participant interaction is not necessary to stimulate your participants, especially if there has been a break or if beverages are available just before or at the beginning of the session.

149. In the mid-afternoon, the primary concern is duration, especially if the participants have been involved in earlier sessions. You as instructor or presenter need to call it quits just before everyone runs out of steam rather than just after.

When participants have had enough for one day, their mental energies start to flag. I find a net negative effect on learning if the session goes on too long. Information bounces back or off the participants, and then may even become meaningless and start to reflect negatively on the content received earlier in the day.

150. If you push your participants past their limit, you and they will gain nothing. So end your session at or just before the time your participants' minds shut down. They will retain more and benefit more. Sticking to an arbitrary time ending if the participants energies are spent will not serve you or them well.

3:30 to 5 p.m. Late afternoon time frame.

If your participants are coming from work to a class or have been involved in another activity during the day, the late afternoon time frame is sometimes seen as a fresh start to the rest of the day.

But if your participants have been in sessions all day, the late afternoon time frame is a tough one for conducting a session.

In some cases, of course, your participants are so attracted and interested in your subject matter that the time of day is not so important to them as your content.

151. But be aware of limited energies and plan accordingly. That may mean conducting the session as a discussion or interactive session, keeping them talking, and making your points in the context of a group discussion. If you have content to share, it may mean doing a fast-run presentation, aware that your participants' limited energies will allow them to absorb a quick 35-minute presentation better than a longer 55-minute presentation.

If group activities stimulate energies, great. But if they are a further drain on already diminishing energies, you might want to make those group activities short. Changing techniques more quickly and using more varied techniques also may help your participants. For example, you might want a short introduction, followed by a quick question-and-answer session, then a three-minute video, then a 10-minute break, then a group discussion.

6 to 10 p.m. Evening sessions

Evening sessions are a mixed bag. If your participants are coming from work for your class, then this is a fresh start for them. On the other hand, physical energies during the evening will be more limited than they are during the day, and you should take that into account.

152. A mixture of content and group interaction and discussion is optimal for evening sessions. Using three to five different teaching techniques during the evening time frame will help keep participants' attention and assist in their learning.

The time of day when your class or session meets makes a difference in your participants' attention and involvement. By adjusting your strategies for each time frame, you can maximize the retention and satisfaction of your participants.

You may be able to recall your own learning experiences during different time frames. I have taken an art appreciation course with slides in a darkened room at 7:45 a.m. (a bad idea) but I also admire my graduate school professors who managed to keep a class of adults interested and active during the weekday evening after a tough day at work. Whatever the situation, work the time frame to your advantage.

Day and Night of the Week

Unlike the time of day, the day or night of the week does not directly influence a participant's learning or retention.

The day of the week and the night of the week do affect attendance for your class or session. If you can choose the day or night to offer your class or session, here are some guidelines.

153. Day of the week. There are no general trends as to the day of the week that is best for a session. If you are working with a given profession or work group, often one day or some days of the week may be better than others, depending on the profession. For example, the best day of the week for nurses to attend a seminar differs from the best day of the week for doctors. The best day of the week for hairstylists to attend a seminar is Sunday because most salons are closed, and they won't lose any business by attending a seminar on a Sunday. So if you are working with a given profession or industry group, find out what the typical schedule is to determine the best day of the week.

154. Night of the week. If you are offering a class or session on a night, some general principles do apply in many situations. The best night for classes is Tuesday. Tuesday night is followed by Thursday, then Monday, and then Wednesday. For Monday, there is Monday night football in the fall, now a consideration in the United States. Wednesday may be church night in a number of communities around the country, and thus other nights afford better attendance.

After the week nights is Sunday night, which a number of programmers have found to be a good night, especially for single people. That is followed by Friday night. The worst night of the week to offer a class or session is Saturday night.

155. Weekend times. Some general guidelines for offering sessions and classes on the weekend are based on programs' experiences over the years. The best weekend time is Sunday afternoon, followed by Sunday night, then Friday night, then Saturday afternoon, then Saturday morning, and tied for the worst time of the weekend to offer a session or class is Sunday morning (with the exception of religious classes, of course) and Saturday night. Middle-aged adults prefer Saturday afternoon over weekend nights, and sometimes even weekday nights, as the baby boom generation starts to tire earlier in the evening.

To reiterate, the day of the week, night of the week, or weekend time a class or session is offered does not so much affect the actual learning gained by the participants, but it can affect the attendance at your class or session.

The Seasons of Learning

The season of the year your session takes place may influence the behavior of your participants in the program.

For sessions in summer, for example, the participants are apt to be more relaxed, verging on overrelaxed, often accompanied by a shorter cognitive attention span and an eagerness to be more active and spend more time out of doors.

The season of the year affects participant interest in the subject and attentiveness in the session.

People are interested in different subjects at different times of the year. More people are interested in taking photography classes in the fall, for instance, than at other times of the year. Secretarial courses receive more attention in the spring than during the other seasons.

For seminars and conferences on professional development, the work cycle for each profession or industry will influence not only the attendance but also the attention given by the participants.

A person attending a session during or just before a particularly hectic period at work, for instance, will be more on edge, less relaxed, and often retain less because of the distraction from work.

On the other hand, a program just before a major work period on improving performance related to that work will engender not only greater attendance but also greater attention on the part of the participants. Timing programs to coincide with greater interest on the part of the participants attracts more attendance and attention.

Chapter 11
Controlling The
Natural Factors

From the natural environment's effect on the time of your session, whether it be time of day, day of week, or month of year, we move to the natural environment's effect on your meeting room and ways you can deal successfully with the natural aspects of light, noise, and temperature.

Lighting

"Lights up" is the word for illuminating your learning room. Too much artificial light is rarely a problem, but there are thousands of cases in which too little artificial light is a problem.

If you are meeting in a room that has too little light, try hard to do something about it. Find out if someone can turn up the lights. Bring in a couple of standing lamps from home if you need to. Ask about getting the room switched. Open the shades if there are windows, and your meeting is during the day.

Sunlight or natural light can be a problem. Glare, looking into the sun, and the sun's rays can all sometimes make it more difficult to see. The sun's rays change during the course of your session. For all these reasons, monitor the sunlight in your room carefully throughout your session. If that is a hassle, close the blinds if there is enough artificial sunlight in the room. A little sunlight perks people up, but too much can be a big distraction.

In many instances, the lighting in the room is fine. Just turn all the lights on. But most of the problems with lighting in learning situations come from not readjusting the lighting after an audio-visual presentation.

Here are some things to watch out for.

156. Keep yourself in the limelight. If there is a dilemma of whether to have yourself in the lighted part of the room or your participants, the winner is you. If you are visible and in the light, your participants will be able to see you and the presentation will be livelier. If you are in a dimmed light situation, the grayness of the visual dampens their receptivity to what you are saying.

157. Darken the lights only for a moment. If you need to darken the room for a slide presentation or other reason, keep the lights on until then. Don't darken the room beforehand.

Instead, before the session starts, play with the lights and learn the lighting controls. If you have a choice, darken the room most where your screen is.

If controlling both the lights and your session is not possible, then ask a participant or a helper to handle the lights for you.

158. Bring the lights up. This is the most common mistake with lighting: we don't bring the lights up immediately after a visual. Instead participants are left in the dark, and we proceed with our presentation, and it loses effect. Bring the lights up as soon as your audio-visual portion is over.

If you are doing more than one audio-visual segment, bring the lights up after each segment or rearrange your presentation to combine all the audio-visual presentations in one time frame. The critical point is not to leave your participants in the dark. That will diminish your presentation and their learning.

If you want to investigate lighting specifications further, The Lighting Handbook of the Illuminating Engineering Society is cited by Reginald Foucar-Szocki in Improving Conference Design and Outcomes. He says the handbook "has a complete listing of recommended footcandle levels for every room, ranging from a lecture room (70 footcandles) to a classroom with a chalkboard (150 footcandles)."

We may not have much control over the lighting of the room, but we have a little control. Use as much flexibility as the situation allows to maximize the artificial light in the room. A dimmed environment will mean a substantially dimmed learning outcome for your participants. Keep the lights on.

Noise

Nothing destroys a good session like outside noise. Take whatever precautionary measures you can to prevent outside noise from interfering. If it happens, seek to diminish the effect.

If you are in a room with permanent walls, you are in good shape. But if there are partitions for walls, such as in a ballroom in a hotel, check out the partitions. If the partitions are solid, you are in fairly good shape. Solid partitions are one-inch or so thick and have more sound resistance. If the partition is a single piece of material and is sliding, then you may have a noise problem.

Here are some things to do to reduce or deal with noise problems.

159. Speak to your next-door neighbor. If a session is scheduled next to yours, go over before either session starts and introduce yourself in a friendly way.

Ask whether the person is using a microphone. If he or she is using a mike and you are not, your participants may be at a disadvantage.

In a friendly sort of way, let the other instructor or presenter know that if you are creating any noise problems, that he or she should feel free to let you know. This is a positive "take the hint" message, and most other instructors or presenters understand that it works both ways. It also makes the other person conscious of a noise interference problem.

160. Position yourself near the potential noise problem. If your room has a sliding partition that isn't a solid wall or your room is near a kitchen or some other potential noise problem, rearrange the room to position yourself near the noise. This is exactly the opposite of what one would think to do, but it works. By putting yourself away from the noise, you are not affected, but your participants are.

By positioning yourself near the noise, you are less affected because you are speaking and you are concentrating on your material. In most cases with good instructors and presenters, the world could be coming to an end and the presenters would be so engrossed in the session they would not notice.

But your participants are not so engrossed, and they do notice the difference, even little differences. So put yourself near the source of the noise.

161. If you are into your session and an outside noise begins to interfere, you can joke about it once or twice. But don't refer to it repeatedly. That only distracts your participants and calls attention to the interference.

Instead, if the noise persists, let your participants know you are aware of the noise and that it is not something you can do anything about. Ask your audience just to ignore the noise as much as possible and concentrate on the matter at hand.

In this way, you have given your participants "permission" to ignore the noise. Sometimes we can block out a good deal of outside noise when we put our minds to it.

162. In the worst case scenario, of course, you can go to the source of the noise and ask for it to be reduced. If you are in a hotel, for example, and it is the hotel staff making the noise, you should be given utmost and prompt response. Another presenter may not take kindly to the request, but you have a 50-50 chance of succeeding, and usually not much to lose.

Outside noise is always a troubling and unpleasant intrusion. Do what you can before your session starts to anticipate and reduce outside noise. If it interferes with your session, acknowledge that with your participants and help them concentrate as best they can on your session.

Temperature

The physical comfort of the room is a factor in how well we are able to listen, interact, and stay focused.

The basic rule in gauging whether your participants are too hot or too cold is that your opinion does not count. As the instructor or presenter, you may be standing up, have more air space around you than your participants, may be at a different end of the room, and you are absorbed in your presentation and facilitating the discussion. Unfortunately, your participants are less absorbed, and temperature affects them.

Here are some tips in battling the ever present temperature control problem.

163. Unlike other physical aspects of your learning environment, temperature is an individual matter. One person may be hot while another cold.

The best advice I have heard has come from seminar guru Anver Suleiman. He urges that participants be given a list of suggestions before the educational meeting or program starts, perhaps with a confirmation statement. One of the suggestions that always should be included is to encourage each participant to wear "layered clothing." This means wear or bring a sweater, jacket, suitcoat, or sweater vest. Then if the participants are too hot, they can shed some clothing; and if the room is too cool, they can keep the sweater on. In this way you as instructor or presenter shift the responsibility for proper temperature control to your participants. You may still have to deal with any failures or excesses in heating or cooling equipment, but you have restricted your responsibility to a much broader range of temperatures and encouraged your participants to anticipate the situation.

Ironically, more of your participants may be too cold during the summer and too hot during the winter because they have dressed for outside rather than inside temperatures. Again, a written suggestion on dress will help head off those kinds of problems.

164. Ask your participants. At least once or twice during your session, particularly just before the first break, ask your participants about the temperature. Then you have the first break to try to make some adjustments.

165. Empower your participants to take action. Allow your participants to make temperature adjustments. Again, they are more aware of and sensitive to the situation than you are. Let them adjust the temperature controls. That again takes the responsibility out of your hands and into theirs.

166. In "How to Conduct Training Seminars," Lawrence Munson says that as the temperature rises above 72 degrees, lethargy and drowsiness increase and the quality of group discussion decreases. "Seminar leaders prefer the temperature to be slightly on the cool side. But please don't go below 66 degrees—or you again begin to lose the group," he notes.

Check out your temperature controls for the room beforehand. If the temperature control is for your room only, you can control it. If it is for the total building, then meet the climate control specialist for the building and get an extension number before the session starts. Opening windows can be a mixed blessing; so monitor the situation if you are opening windows to adjust the temperature. The best preventive measure is to inform your participants ahead of time to bring clothing that can respond to their need to be warmer or cooler.

Chapter 12
Planning Tips to Start

The effect of the natural environment such as time of day, lighting, and temperature, are all to be considered as part of the planning process for your session.

While you are planning your content and subject matter for the course, your participants subconsciously are engaged in a preliminary process leading up to your session.

The days before your session can be used to send messages that will increase your participants' readiness, eagerness, and even satisfaction.

You can create a positive learning environment before your session begins.

Creating a welcoming environment

The learning environment begins as soon as the learner registers or commits to attending your program. Adults, while self-directed, self-motivated, and seemingly independent and in control, actually experience a sense of unease and uncertainty each time they become involved in a program.

We wonder whether we will be able to master the subject, we wonder about our participation in the group, and we wonder if there will be other people like ourselves in the group.

Several years ago when working on an earlier book, "How to Teach Adults," I took my vacation as usual in northern Wisconsin. While there I registered for a CPR class meeting in an elementary school. I walked in and, of course, knew no one there. And a little feeling of unease and uncertainty ensued. I remember thinking that if I am writing a book on teaching adults and feel a little uncertain, then it may be a universal feeling among all learners, regardless of their experience or outward demeanor. Much to his credit, the CPR instructor immediately dispelled the uneasy feeling for everyone in the class with his introductions. A good teacher or presenter can do that. You also can help do that with a welcoming environment.

Here are some ideas for creating a welcoming environment:

167. If days or weeks elapse between registration and your session, a confirmation letter not only reaffirms the person's attendance but also welcomes the person to the program, restates the program's objectives, and assures the person that he or she will benefit from the experience.

168. For hotel meetings and conferences, a welcoming note put in the message box of your participants when they check in is a pleasant and welcome surprise. After a day of travelling, you are reassured by such a note that you are in the right place, that everything is all right, and that you are welcomed.

169. Send readings in advance. For some programs, it will prepare your participants both mentally and with substantive information if readings are sent in advance. Those readings can be a complete set of handouts, books, or publications. Or it could be simply an article or two-page summary. Receiving readings ahead of time indicates your program is well-planned and something you take seriously and hope your participants will as well.

If you do send out readings, clarify in writing whether the participants are to have read everything before they come and whether they should bring the materials with them to your session. Let them know whether reading the material is critical or just an added feature.

170. Direction signs. Signs to your meeting place lessen anxiety and create reassurance. It is more than just arriving at the right spot at the right time: it is arriving without stress, inconvenience, and in the best frame of mind for entering the learning situation. The more signs, the better. Some signs, such as on the hotel marquee or in the airport, also enhance the prestige of your program.

Put a sign outside the door to your meeting room. Include the title of the session and the starting and ending times.

If you are in a hotel or large building, a directional sign helping participants find the right corridor or area is also appreciated.

When someone walks into your meeting room, what are the visual clues? What tells the participant that this is going to be a pleasant experience?

Let's look at those two words. First, more and more we are coming to understand that learning situations are not isolated identifiable interludes between real life, but that they are real life and are interpreted as "experiences." An experience is something that happens to or involves you. Your participants do not judge a session simply on its cognitive merits, but they evaluate the time spent as a total experience. Many aspects, from introductions to interaction with others, go into making up a total experience.

By making that experience a "pleasant" one, the participant's learning will be enhanced and advanced. The more pleasant the experience, the more learning can take place.

Visual clues when walking into your meeting room can enhance the experience for your participants.

171. If you have a permanent room, or one in which you can do something to the walls, do something! Put up posters, signs, pictures, or symbols of success, such as:

—Posters with motivational comments
—Pictures that help set a pleasant atmosphere
—Mission statement of your organization
—Pictures of past classes
—Maps, charts, diagrams related to your subject matter

Think about distinguishing your learning environment from just an attractive meeting room environment. Can you make your walls a little more active and interactive? Can you make them "jump" just a little?

172. Welcome banner. Create a large welcome banner with a dot matrix printer and post it across the wall.

173. Create a "welcome overhead" and put it on about 10 minutes before session starts. A large and colorful overhead will create a picture on the wall, welcoming your participants.

174. Simply write "Welcome" on the flip chart. Use the flip chart as a welcoming device.

Testimonials

Testimonials increase your participants' learning. Testimonials are comments from past participants about their experience and how your session helped them.

Testimonials let your current participants know others have benefitted from your course or program. They also point to previous participants as being successful with the implication that your current participant can be successful, too. This is particularly true when the testimonial is from someone with whom a current participant can affiliate, someone like the current participant. Sometimes that means a good testimonial can best come from your "common" or "ordinary" participants, not people with name recognition.

Here are some tips in using testimonials.

175. Put a testimonial in your brochure or promotional copy. It works wonders.

176. Use a testimonial as a motivator by putting the comment on a poster on the wall, or in an overhead, or with the person's picture.

177. Use a testimonial as a motivator halfway through the session or course by casually mentioning the person and repeating the testimonial.

Here are ways to gather and compose testimonials.

178. The best source of testimonials is your evaluation forms. The last question on the evaluation form should be: "Other comments or testimonial." Then after leaving plenty of space, preferably with lines for easier writing, note "If the above is a testimonial, may we use it in our publicity? _____ yes _____ no. If yes, please sign here" with a line for the signature.

You need only a few good testimonials for your course or session. Your evaluation forms will generate those testimonials.

179. You do need permission in writing to use the testimonial. That's why the evaluation form has a place for the signature. Keep the testimonials on file in case you ever are challenged about the validity or permission to use a given testimonial.

180. You can edit testimonials. You don't have to use the whole testimonial. You cannot add language or words, but you can select only certain words, as long as the meaning or intent remains the same.

In fact, in most cases, you want to edit the testimonial. The best testimonial is short, crisp, and has some snappy language. So within the participant's copy look for that short, crisp and snappy phrase.

181. If someone writes you a letter or gives you an oral comment that would make a great testimonial, write it down immediately. Send it to the person, and ask him or her to sign a permission form and send it right back to you.

182. When you use the testimonial, always use the person's name. Testimonials without names on them conjure up the possibility they are fake or made up. Initials are not that great either. Use the person's full name.

No one needs to know the person giving the testimonial to believe that person. The believability is in the person's name, real, not made up. Sometimes identification is helpful, but it is not necessary. Again, people do not have to know the person to find the testimonial credible.

183. Occasionally someone might actually try to call a person giving a testimonial. Give out the person's phone number unless there is some confidentiality consideration. This is a positive indication on the part of the person wanting to talk to a previous participant. Sometimes others can represent and praise your session or course better than you can.

Testimonials are no-cost learning enhancers. They are commonly seen as ways to get people into a course or program, but they are much more than that. They help motivate people already in your program or course. They point to success. They are proof that others just like your current participants have succeeded.

Sprinkle one or two testimonials throughout your course or program.

Part V
Learning Mediums

Chapter 13
Setting the Mood

Learning Mediums

A teacher or presenter can encourage learning by using physical aids we have called Teaching Tools in this book.

As learning moves from a teacher- or presenter-centered approach to a participant- or learner-centered approach, a growing number of physical aids are being developed or discovered that enhance learning by directly affecting the participants.

Learning Mediums differ from Teaching Tools. Teaching tools help the teacher present information, clarify a point, or illustrate an idea. Learning mediums, on the other hand, have a different role. Learning mediums occupy a middle ground between the presenter and participant. They often surround or envelop the participant. Sometimes they are the substance through which an effect is transmitted.

Because no term has yet been coined to define them, we have invented the term "learning mediums" here to describe these physical aids to learning. One definition and use of the word medium is "the message; it is the medium that shapes and controls the scale and form of human association and action; a medium is an extension of ourselves," according to Marshall McLuhan.

To differentiate the concept from "media," which is commonly thought of as direct communication, usually involving sight and sound, we use a less common but equally correct plural form of mediums for these physical aids.

Some of the learning mediums described here help set the stage or prepare participants for learning. Others are used during the activity, event, class or session. Most affect a participant's sensory system or cues in some way. Almost all have a subtle or subconscious rather than an overt or explicit effect—that is, few participants will attribute a competency learned to the flowers in the room.

Almost all of the learning mediums described here have been adapted specifically to the learning situation in just the last few years. Certainly more learning mediums will be invented or adopted in the next few years.

View the learning mediums offered here as choices and alternatives. Use them as you see fit, as often or as sparingly as appropriate for your learning situations. They are not advocated with equal intensity or as a group. As we discover more about learning mediums and understand more fully their effect, those recommendations will evolve.

For now, enjoy discovering and trying the first set of learning mediums. Maybe you can even help develop others.

Music

Playing music before your session starts helps get your participants into a learning mode in at least two ways.

First, it breaks the awkward silence. You know, the instructor is shuffling papers, a few people are pouring coffee, and the rest are sitting staring ahead. Music breaks the awkward silence.

Second, some kinds of music actually can help put people into a learning mode. The Lind Institute in San Francisco, for example, has tapes of classical music constructed with a certain number of beats per minute. This timing is supposed to be the same as our internal "clock," and helps put participants into a learning mode.

The Lind tapes differ noticeably from standard classical music in terms of the effect on participants. I have sat in a seminar where regular classical music was played, and it wasn't the same.

Don't expect everyone to notice the music. It has a more subtle effect. Most won't consciously notice it. Some will think it is being piped in over the hotel's loudspeaker system. Only a few will ask what it is you are playing.

Here are some tips for using music to enhance learning.

184. Play the tapes before the session starts. They can also be turned on during breaks, and even after the end of the session as people leave. But the biggest effect is before the session.

185. Adjust the volume. It should be background music, not loud enough to "listen" to or obstruct conversations.

186. As more people enter the room, the participant noise increases and you will need to turn up the volume.

187. Be sure to stop the tape before the session starts.

188. Bring extra batteries for the cassette player.

189. A small cassette player running on batteries works well. Also, if you purchase a reasonably priced player, you won't be heartbroken if it is damaged while transporting it to the session.

For more information on the Lind tapes, write The Lind Institute, P.O. Box 14487, San Francisco, CA 94114.

Flowers

In "Passion for Excellence," Nancy Austin and Tom Peters talk about the most successful car dealership in Dallas. The most striking feature on the showroom floor is not the new luxury cars but the large floral display in the middle of the showroom. Austin and Peters say that flowers help create a good atmosphere.

Since reading that several years ago, I have tried in different ways to use flowers as a visual and somewhat olfactory aid in setting the learning environment.

Flowers have a calming, engaging, and spritely effect on a group. They are an excellent visual aid in creating a good learning environment.

Here are some ways you can use flowers.

190. At the head table. Put a floral bouquet on the table or the stand in front of the room. Because everyone can see the bouquet throughout your presentation, the flowers get maximum exposure. They provide a colorful yet nondistracting background and convey a "happy message."

191. Registration at conferences. During a seminar I recommended flowers and one of the seminar participants was on the conference committee for the Rhode Island Association for Adult Education.

By coincidence, I was asked to be a speaker at the conference. When I arrived at the registration table, there was a big bouquet of flowers. During my session, I asked the conference attendees, "What was the first thing you noticed when you came to the conference?'' And everyone said it was the flowers.

What a nice greeting to come to a conference and have a bouquet of flowers as part of the welcome.

192. Give the flowers as a prize. After your meeting is almost over, you can use the flowers as a door prize or winner's reward for a good idea. It also saves you the time and trouble of hauling the flowers home after the session. The participants always like winning something, and it is an extra way to use your bouquet.

193. Try buying an inexpensive arrangement. Bouquets can be expensive when ordered from a florist, but there are alternatives. One of the ways you can save money is to buy a small bouquet from the grocery store or discount store for less than the price of a florist's arrangement.

For one seminar I bought an inexpensive bouquet, put it in an ice chest to keep it cool, and then drove six hours for the seminar the next day. My colleague thought that was going to great lengths for the floral touch, but it saved money.

194. Steal one from the hotel. If you are presenting for a meeting in a nice hotel, see if there is a flower in your room or if one comes with room service. A number of hotels put a single flower in a little vase on the tray with room service.

I've taken the flower and vase off the room service tray before my meeting and placed them on the head table for the day. Then I left them at the end of the seminar for the hotel again. I got a free flower, the hotel got its little vase back, and the flower had a great day.

Flowers provide a special touch for a learning environment and are just part of the mix of environmental aids that can help set a positive and welcoming atmosphere for your learning session.

Chapter 14
Making Participants Feel Special

Presents

Presents for your participants are an unexpected pleasure. Few participants come to an educational session expecting to receive a gift. Competition for presents not only immediately gears up an audience, but also subtly lets them know the topic being addressed is important. And presents give you a great opportunity for humor.

Presents should be an "extra." They should not be something a participant might feel everyone in the session should receive. For example, you wouldn't want to make a handout into a present. A handout would be something everyone should get.

Try these tips in using presents for your participants.

195. Presents should be cheap. Not inexpensive, but recognizably cheap. You don't want to give something of exceptionally high value because that disappoints the participants who do not receive such a present. I wouldn't give out a $100 manual, for example, as a present during a seminar. It might create envious and unhealthy feelings among all the rest of the participants. No one feels slighted if someone else gets an inexpensive present, however.

196. Presents should err on the side of novelty items. Novelty items help establish a fun atmosphere and thus facilitate discussion, group thinking, and creativity, all important in learning. In many cases a little levity enhances the learning situation.

One of my favorite "presents for participants" stores is Mr. Bulky's, a confectioner with a wide variety of candy I can't imagine anyone buying: candy in the shape of vegetables, monsters, famous people, and other unusual shapes. Baseball cards are good in the spring, but make sure they have gum with them.

197. Standard office items can be turned into novelty items with the turn of a phrase. Our LERN pens and pencils are never just LERN pens and pencils. They are always the "coveted" LERN pencils and the pens "not available in shops and stores."

198. Presents should vary by the type of audience. You know the characteristics of your group, so tailor the presents for them.

And some groups are more serious than others. My all-time really big prize goes over well for recreation- and leisure-minded groups. Billed as "the complete indoor recreation center," it is a Nerf ball, that small spongy basketball, and hoop, which fits easily into a briefcase.

Presents for participants have several serious uses for you as a teacher or presenter.

199. Opening up discussion and generating questions. In launching any educational session, one effective technique is to encourage participants to ask questions. Questions get them involved, make them think, and let you know where to take your comments.

Because inviting questions at the beginning of a session often results in lots of silence and reluctance, the presents bring the questions out much faster. So for the first five questions from participants, offer a present. After the first person receives a present, the questions flow quickly.

200. Generating ideas in group discussions. Some great ideas can come out of group discussions, and the group discussion participants can be further motivated with a "competition" for great ideas.

Have your participants break into groups to generate ideas. Then have them select the best idea, and the participant with that idea wins a prize.

You also can have a grand prize for the best idea overall. Either you can select the best idea overall, or have the group vote.

201. Recognize individual achievement. You can use your presents as spontaneous responses to good ideas or contributions from your participants. This not only gives the participant a good feeling for a well-deserved contribution but also lets the other participants know what you value as a good idea. It also subtly stimulates them to be involved and make contributions as well.

202. It creates variety in your instruction. If you are doing a course or class that meets over several dates, introducing a little variety into each session helps keep the participants returning in an expecting and eager mode.

Dishing out presents every time you meet will quickly become old hat. But using presents during one of your class meetings injects a little unexpectedness into the session and mixes things up a bit. It is a good idea for one meeting in a series.

Presents for participants are learning aids. They help generate questions. They get people involved early on in your session. They are useful in making group discussions more productive. They reward individuals for contributions to the session, and they create variety for those classes and courses that have multiple meetings. Finally, giving presents to participants is another way for you to show your respect for them and your wish for them to enjoy your session. Subconsciously participants may feel that you as a teacher or presenter care about serving them and making their learning experience a good one.

For all these reasons, giving presents to participants is another positive way to energize your learning environment.

Ribbons

Ribbons are special. I used to think ribbons were just for important people and leaders of educational events. In the last few years my thinking has changed entirely. I think everyone should have a ribbon. And ribbons will have an ever more important role in educational events.

If we change our thinking about ribbons from a recognition for the few to a recognition for the many, some exciting new features of ribbons become apparent.

Ribbons have these important uses for participants.

• They make people feel good. Everyone feels good about having a ribbon. Even when everyone else has a ribbon on, the individual still feels good. So ribbons are an easy and effective way of making people feel special.

At our last conference, we introduced "Five year" ribbons for participants who had been members of our association for five years or more. We thought they would be delighted. They were, but they also wanted more. Several asked that next year we have "10 year" ribbons. That kind of positive response indicates a sense of pride and also helps build one's organization.

• Ribbons distinguish people. Increasingly, segmenting and serving your various markets are important for successful educational meetings. At every educational event today, different kinds of people attend. You have newcomers, old-timers, people with different interests, different geography, and other demographic differences.

Different colors of ribbons for different types of participants give each participant a feeling of individuality. When participants wear more than one ribbon—a newcomer ribbon, plus a ribbon for their location (hometown, county, state or province, country), suddenly you can tell a lot about another participant just by seeing the colors of the ribbons. So ribbons are a way of identifying people and they also create a sense of individuality for the person wearing them.

• Ribbons help people network. The identifying characteristics of ribbons mean that participants can network with others easily. People can find not only others with something in common, but also those with different interests or areas of experience. Because networking at educational sessions is growing more important, you can help facilitate that activity with ribbons.

Here are some kinds of things to have ribbons for.

* Attendance: First-time attendees, previous attendees, five-year, 10-year veterans

* Geography: Hometown, county, state or province, or country ribbons

* Work: Job position, type of organization, company or institutional affiliation

* Interest areas.

The effectiveness of ribbons for conferences has led some to try them for seminars and small group activities as well.

Ribbons are special because they make people feel special. Previously ribbons distinguished the few leaders, presenters and special guests. With the trend toward customer service and greater inclusion of participants, ribbons can make all your participants feel special. In addition, their identification usage and networking value mean that ribbons will become an increasingly more integral part of the educational meeting.

Name tags

Name tags are important for several reasons. One, your participants get them at the beginning of your session, and anything that happens in the beginning is important for setting the learning stage. Two, name tags are another way the image of your session is presented. The kind of name tag you have tells the participants something about what they can expect. Three, the name tag has the participant's name on it, and anything with a person's name is treated with particular attention.

So name tags help set the stage and welcome participants. But name tags also have been a source of frustration for educational and meeting planners. There doesn't seem to be one right name tag. Each kind seems to be wrong for someone.

Here are some of your name tag choices.

• Stick-on name tags. Stick-on name tags are inexpensive and easy to use. The name is written with a felt-tip marker. They are good for one time meetings and seminars, for large crowds, and for low-cost events.

Stick-on name tags are usually one-time only. If the event has several meetings to it, the stick-on name tags won't last longer than one-time. Because they do stick to clothes, some people may be concerned about the adhesive on their clothes.

• Pin name tags. Pin name tags are usually a plastic case with a pin that sticks through one's clothes. They are good for events that have more than one meeting, they are widely used, and you can get them in different sizes. The name can be individually written or printed with a computer.

Pin name tags put holes in clothing. Participants in business dress may find this unappealing.

• Clip-on name tags. Clip-on name tags have the same benefits as the pin name tags, except they don't put holes in clothing.

The clip-on name tags go well with suits, and clip on to either a suit pocket or a lapel. They do not go well with blouses, sweaters and dresses without pockets or lapels.

• Rope name tags. Rope name tags have the plastic case just like pin and clip-on name tags, but instead of the pin or clip, a string goes around the participant's neck. The rope name tag does not ruin business clothes and does not depend on a pocket or lapel. Everyone has a neck.

The rope name tag works functionally. The problem is more in the acceptance by participants. A number of U.S. participants report feeling like a domesticated animal with the rope around the neck. The rope name tag is not widely used in the United States, but is more common in Canada, for example.

• Pin/clip-on name tag. The name tag has the plastic case and then has both a pin and a clip-on. Thus, if you are wearing good business clothes, you can use the clip-on. And if you are wearing clothes without a lapel or pocket, you can use the pin. For events that last several days, this kind works with different outfits every day.

It is innovative and works well, and many recommend it. It comes in two sizes.

• Magnetic name tags. Recently magnetic name tags have been introduced. The magnet holds the name tag to your clothing. It does not require a lapel and does not puncture the clothing.

• Some or all choices. Some organizations lay out several choices of name tags at educational meetings.

Allowing your participants to choose the name tag holder reduces any complaints about name tags and is good customer service. It does mean that your printed name tags cannot be put into the plastic case beforehand, and thus makes registration a little more time-consuming.

Choose the name tag that fits your audience, your budget, your desired level of quality, and your educational event. Omnipresent, name tags are a visible aspect of your educational meeting and should contribute to your session's success.

Chapter 15
Creating Sensory Experience

The senses that affect one's learning are not just the visual and auditory senses. We are discovering that the other senses can assist, or detract from, learning as well. Here we explore just a few ways in which touch, taste and even smell can influence one's learning.

Smell

Malcolm Knowles, the father of adult education, tells the story of an adult educator who converted an old elementary school into an adult learning center. The director was just finishing cleaning the windows before the center opened when two high school drop-outs walked by. They saw the sign saying the building was now an adult learning center and stopped on the sidewalk and stared. Finally one of them walked up to the building and sniffed the front door. Then he walked back to his friend on the sidewalk. "Still smells like a school to me," he said, and they walked off.

When I heard Malcolm tell that story, I thought it was a great allegory about image and marketing to adult learners. Which it is. Years later I discovered that the story is also about the physical sensation of smell and its effect on learning.

You can enhance your learning environment with smell, and negative smells have a detrimental effect on learning.

What influence do smells have? Negative smells, such as institutional smells from cleaning fluids, bring up past images of negative experiences, such as experiences in schools, hospitals, and other institutional settings. On the other hand, pleasant smells bring to mind pleasant experiences, such as being at home, being with family and friends, having a good time, being out of doors, eating great food.

Some smells, negative to most of us, may be attractive to particular audiences because they evoke a positive image. For example, when hairstylists attend seminars the instructor can notice an immediate and noticeable rise in energy and interest when ammonia is opened and released in the air. To most of us, this is an awful smell. But to a hairstylist, it is the smell of business and of money.

Although the research on creating a positive olfactory environment is in its early stages, there are already a number of ways you can use smell to energize the learning environment.

Here are some tips collected so far.

203. Bake a pie. If you are in a building with a kitchen, bake an apple pie in the oven at 200 degrees for about four hours. By turning the oven on at warm for a long time the smell permeates the building. This has been used successfully for open houses, first night of sessions, registration times, and others.

204. Vanilla. Real estate agents often put a dab of vanilla on a light bulb. The smell of vanilla then fills the room, creating a pleasant odor.

205. Potpourri. Boutiques and novelty stores sell spices in little jars which can be lit underneath and spread a variety of different smells throughout the room.

206. Fireplaces. Most meeting rooms don't have fireplaces. But if you are meeting in a home or retreat setting and there is one, the smell of a wood fire in a fireplace is great, even in summer.

207. Incense. Used "lightly," perhaps an hour before the session starts, an incense stick is another choice to consider.

208. Coffee. Make a pot of coffee. For many just the smell of coffee brewing is a pleasant "wake up."

209. Air spray. If your meeting room has an unpleasant smell, consider an air spray to neutralize the negative smell.

You may well be able to think of others. Psychologists and those who study human behavior indicate that smell plays a much larger role in our lives than we admit. The modern societal concept of eliminating smell may not be so appropriate as changing the smell to create an environment that conjures up positive images and feelings and sets the stage for enhanced learning.

Food and drink

Food and drink can facilitate and boost learning. And when meals are too heavy, food can be a detriment to learning.

A little bit of food and drink can go a long way to create a positive learning environment, generate group cohesiveness, and create participant involvement and satisfaction.

Here are some positive ways you can use food and drink to stimulate learning.

210. If you are teaching a multisession class or course, desserts, especially accompanied by coffee and tea, can be a welcome surprise for your participants. The dessert and coffee will prompt more community or group feeling. In some classes participants take turns and bring a dessert each week.

211. Mints. A simple mint, in each person's place after lunch or after a break, is a little extra that almost everyone appreciates. Hard mints are inexpensive, pack and travel easily, and are unlikely to spoil. Put one on the table in front of each participant, or on each person's chair, either after lunch or during a break. People also appreciate the personal attention you are providing them.

212. Morning coffee and tea. A necessity for almost every gathering is access to coffee and tea in the morning. For an added touch, have a pitcher of orange juice available.

More meeting sponsors are serving fruit in the morning although some fruits are easier to eat than others.

213. There is some movement toward bagels and fruit muffins and away from doughnuts and pastry. You can save on costs by ordering fewer baked goods and then cutting them in half. Your participants won't mind and can take seconds if they want, and you will save money.

214. Lunches. One of the more common mistakes in all-day seminars or conferences is to serve a heavy lunch. Heavy lunches make participants drowsy, their energies flag, and they are less able to concentrate in the afternoon.

Here are some suggestions to make your lunch a learning lunch, one which will enhance rather than detract from learning.

215. Eliminate heavy desserts. Don't serve pies, cakes, brownies or other heavy desserts. They ruin the after-lunch attention span. Instead, have ice cream or sherbet and possibly a side cookie.

216. Choose light lunches. Here are some light lunches that will keep your participants alert.

—Soup and sandwiches
—Deli plates of cheese, meats, and breads
—Chef salads
—Rice instead of potatoes or pasta
—Vegetables
—Fruit cups— in summer, fruit plates

Menu items that detract from learning include meat, gravy and potatoes. If your audience won't eat lighter foods, then work with the kitchen to lessen the portions.

By serving a light rather than a heavy lunch, you often can save money and participants will like the variety or change from the standard luncheon fares. Most important, you will not have left them stuffed and practically unable to learn in the afternoon. If you want your participants to have a good afternoon and use their valuable time best, give them a light lunch.

Food, especially in small doses, is a great stimulator for learning. For your class or session, think about any ways in which you can provide a little food or drink for your participants. They will appreciate it, and their learning will be enhanced.

The morning paper

The morning paper is a daily ritual for many people. The morning paper orients us to the world: it is a wake up mechanism; and it gets the brain cells active again.

Regardless of the time of day your session begins, a "paper" can help orient your participants to your session, wake them up a bit, and get their brain cells working in the direction of your subject matter.

Put a "morning paper" on the chairs or tables before the participants enter the room. Or hand them to the participants as they enter. This shows you are ready for them and is another welcome sign.

Here are some types of morning papers.

217. Agenda. An excellent learning aid is to provide a copy of the agenda. This helps each participant know what to expect. If you have a session that meets several times, you can have a written agenda for each meeting if you want.

In writing agendas, avoid exact times. For example, 7:15-7:35 p.m. we will discuss _____. This locks in your participants' expectations and limits your flexibility. Often it can be a source of challenge from a participant who wanted the full 12 minutes on section 8, and was not pleased you spent twice as much time as indicated on section 7. So for your own flexibility, leave out exact times on your agenda.

218. Personal note. Nothing works so well as a personal note, even if it isn't really personal. For the first session, write a one or two paragraph personal note to your participants explaining why you wanted to offer this session, what you hope they will get out of it, and that you are glad they came. This helps set the stage for your session and allows you to be friendly and personal.

219. The news. Produce your own news-paper. On just one sheet, type up from three to six newsy items of interest to your participants and relevant to the subject you are addressing.

Something is always happening in your field. Include an anniversary or story. If you have an appropriate cartoon, paste that on. The "news" gives your participants something active to do before your session starts, helps reduce that awkward silence time, and it may stimulate discussion.

Putting some paper in front of the participants as they enter the room is a positive technique to start their thinking about your subject matter, of welcoming them, and giving them something to do before the session. Think of it as your morning newspaper.

Part VI
Conclusion and Further Resources

Chapter 16
Responding To
Your Participants

What we've tried to do in this book is to explore the concept that the physical environment and physical objects do affect learning. One can reduce barriers, stimulate learners' interest, create a learning atmosphere, and complement one's instruction or presentation by using a variety of physical factors.

We proceed from the notion that the participants in your class or session are self-directed and inherently motivated. They are capable of independent learning and acquire the most skills and knowledge, positive attitude, or value changes, when they take charge of their own learning. We as instructors and presenters facilitate that learning, provide information when needed, and also encourage their own exploration and seeking. The best learning is voluntary, self-fulfilling and internally rewarding. Learning that is internally rewarding provides us with continual motivation and interest. Such learning allows us to seek and better retain other learning activities, whether in a formal educational situation or not.

Internally rewarding learning is a fire that when lit, continues to burn. Our role as instructors and presenters is to provide the kindling and coax the flame, being careful not to extinguish it by too much wind or cold water.

Less effective learning is externally motivated, done for corporate (in the broadest sense) reasons that the learner does not fully integrate and embrace. This external learning is more likely to be passive, one-way communication, less interactive, and consequently less valuable. Here learning is seen more like an empty glass to be filled. Here learning is facts and figures, and only facts and figures, often with predetermined outcomes or behaviors.

Our role as instructor or presenter is to enhance the self-fulfilling and internally rewarding learning, recognizing that we (our organization, our company, our community, our society, our group) gain far more from one who is a self-directed and self-motivated learner than we do from one who is a passive reactive student.

Consequently, our role is changing dramatically. We are less and less the purveyor of information, facts, figures, and details. We are more and more the one who relates the information to our learners, who makes mental connections, who fills in the knowledge gaps, who answers questions, who generates discussion, who asks questions not even we can answer.

We are also the ones who ignite the passion, the fascination, the intrigue of our subject or exploration, who can stimulate the learning to continue far beyond our own time-limited and place-limited formal educational session.

And we are also role models. We are the purveyors of hope, the messenger of dreams, of vision, not only for our subject matter and its importance but also for our participants and their importance and their value. We do that most concretely by acting as internally rewarding learners ourselves, by looking for that excitement or new knowledge in our own sessions and most likely finding it in our own participants, seeking to learn from them and by doing so also showing them how they can learn from us and from each other.

This is a more personal kind of learning and instruction or presentation. This is more you-and-me. It is more challenging and more effective. It is also more relevant and pertinent to the challenges and opportunities that we all as citizens, workers, and people face in the 21st century. This is not a vague, touchy-feely approach to a science. Rather, this is a scientific and proven method of getting results.

Here the emphasis is on the learner. Our new role as instructors and presenters is a more personal and participant oriented rather than subject-oriented teaching.

Thus, the physical environment and the physical objects within that environment are not impersonal technological aids for "making people learn," or artificially enlarging that passive receptacle so that more water can be poured into it. These practical tips and techniques are not to replace human interaction, substitute for a more personal style in teaching, or to reinforce one-way communication.

Quite the contrary, the tips and suggestions in this book are to enhance that personal style of teaching, to complement group activities such as brainstorming, small group activities, discussions and Socratic dialogue, to assist you as a facilitator. They are to help kindle the flames of learning. They assist your participants in creating their own learning.

The overriding purpose of this book is for us as instructors and presenters to have a new or renewed sense of how we can positively manipulate our physical learning environment and physical objects to enhance self-directed and participatory learning. With that perspective, then we will find our own ways to modify or massage that physical environment to complement and enhance our teaching and their learning. There are no prescriptions here, but a wealth of alternatives, choices and opportunities.

The more than 200 individual tips, techniques, suggestions, and ideas offered here were generated by dozens of presenters and instructors from all over the world. If you take just one of those tips and use it in your own way, then this book will have achieved its purpose and you will have made a good investment.

We are at the threshold of a new century, a new millennium for our civilization. At the same time, we are on the brink of a new millennium in learning. It is an exciting time.

It is hoped that learning will not be compartmentalized, fact and figured, sterilized, impersonalized, and packaged, complete with numerical measurements and requirements. Instead it will be an open arena, a sand box, a new blank page, an open computer screen, waiting for each one of us to make of it as will most benefit us and our neighbors, creating and revitalizing and planning and visioning that future and that next great exploration. These are exciting times for us as learners and instructors and presenters. It is a time when we can energize the learning environment.

Appendix A
Going Shopping

Shopping for inexpensive, colorful, and slightly offbeat materials can yield results that will help put zip, zing, and a little pizazz in your session.

The best stores for presenters to shop are stationery, discount, candy and toy stores.

Here are my picks on the best items to buy in each store. They are not basic or fundamental supplies. Rather they are additional materials that add extra zip. The lists are not in any priority.

Here are the top things to buy in a stationery store.

1. Art and craft paper, size 10 by 13, especially the metallic paper, for signs.
2. Color coding labels. These are colored dots, good for "voting" on participants' favorite ideas, or sticking on name badges as rewards or special recognition.
3. Poster-perfect project board. Colors that stand out best are hot pink, hot yellow, grey, yellow, and green.
4. Poster board, size 28 by 44. The most unusual and attractive colors are orange, yellow, and light blue.
5. Plastic tube. Put your posters, drawings, charts, and other material in a plastic tube for safekeeping.
6. Colored index cards. The best is the color pack with a mixture of pink, green, salmon, and yellow.
7. Sidewalk chalk. If you have to use a chalkboard, use this huge chalk in pink, yellow, and blue.
8. Industrial strength felt-tip markers. These are jumbo, family-size markers.

9. Mat board. This solid poster board gives you more selections for colors and textures, including soft green, light teal, maroon, wine, rose, sandstone, and brick red.
10. Masking tape. Don't forget a little masking tape for putting up those great ideas on the wall.

Here are the top ideas for things to buy in a toy store:
1. Baseball cards, with gum.
2. Catwoman digital watch; it glows in the dark.
3. Batman chalk.
4. Dinoball; leaping lizards, they're pre-hysterical.
5. Dopey, Bashful, Sneezy, Sleepy, or Happy Seven Dwarfs dolls.
6. Wacky Writer, a motorized writing pen with five hot colors.
7. Ernie's rubber duckie; it floats, it's soft, it's all vinyl
8. Mr. Potato Head.
9. Mrs. Potato Head
10. Jurassic Park putty stickers; if it's not Jurassic Park, it's extinct.

Here are the top items to buy in a candy store.
1. Candy lipstick.
2. Giant bazooka squeeze gum.
3. Chocolate coins;
4. Chocolate tennis balls, footballs, baseballs and soccer balls.
5. Laffy Taffy, in apple, watermelon, lemonade, passion punch or orange flavors.
6. Lemon or orange slices.
7. Jelly belly beans, with pink grapefruit, butterscotch, cantaloupe, buttered popcorn, raspberry, pina colada, orange sherbet, A&W root beer, apricot, or mai-tai flavors.
8. Nerds.
9. Holiday candy when in season, or totally out of season.

Appendix B
Exploring Further
Resources

This book concentrates on the physical aspects of teaching and presenting in an educational session. It was not intended to cover all aspects of teaching and presenting.

Consequently, it is with great pleasure that I am able to introduce and refer you to a select number of the best resources on adult learning and teaching, as seen from my perspective as an adult educator and practitioner in the field of seminars and educational presentations. These references, of course, carry my bias, which is away from both purely academic works and mere technique or style guides, toward those works that are not only practical but also learner-centered and oriented toward educational quality.

They are not additional resources on the physical learning environment. Those sources are provided in the references and bibliography sections of this book.

1. *The Adult Learner, A Neglected Species,* by Malcolm S. Knowles, Revised Edition, Gulf Publishing Company, Houston, 1984. Knowles, sometimes called the "father of adult education," is the foremost advocate of self-directed learning and voluntary learning for adults. His work on adult learning and andragogy, or how one learns, is fundamental to the area of adult learning.

2. *Helping Adults Learn and Change,* by Russell D. Robinson, Omnibook Company, Milwaukee, 1979. Robinson, a pro-

fessor of adult education, has put together one of the more readable and helpful guides for presenters and teachers of adults. The book covers the gamut, from adult motivation and development to teaching techniques and plans, from learning to teaching with clear, crisp outlines and models.

3. *How to Teach Adults,* by William A. Draves, Learning Resources Network (LERN), Manhattan, KS, 1994, Second Edition. The most widely used and popular book on teaching adults, it offers concise and easy-to-read guidelines especially geared for part-time teachers and presenters.

4. *Mastering the Teaching of Adults,* by Jerold Apps, Krieger Publishing, Melbourne, FL, 1990. Apps is one of the more respected adult educators today. His book goes beyond the basics and looks at a more personal and interactive involvement for the teacher or presenter. With the teacher's role moving from information transfer to facilitator, this book is essential to making teaching more meaningful to learners.

5. *Imaginative Events for Training,* by Ken Jones, McGraw-Hill, Inc., New York, NY, 1993. Called a trainer's sourcebook of games, simulations, and role-play exercises, the book includes participation exercises intended to jog minds, challenge routine ideas, encourage innovative thinking, help participants learn to cope with change, and provoke and amuse. It is the latest in a number of fine books on games participants and trainers can play.

References

Chapter 1. The Apex of Learning.
1. *Pyramid Power,* by Max Toth and Greg Nielsen, Destiny Books, Rochester, Vermont, 1985, pages 136-137 on Egyptian priests and the apex.
2. *Pyramids and the Second Reality,* by Bill Schul and Ed Pettit, Fawcett Columbine, New York, 1979, pages 162-163 on the scientific properties of pyramids.
3. *Encyclopaedia Britannica,* Encyclopaedia Britannic, Inc., Chicago, London, Toronto, 1945, Volume 7, pages 737 and 744-745 on the origin of "dunce" and the life of John Duns Scotus.
4. *The Woman's Dictionary of Symbols and Sacred Objects,* by Barbara G. Walker, Harper & Row, Publishers, San Francisco, 1988, page 83 on the history of the apex.

Chapter 2. Learning and Teaching in the 21st Century.
1. *The Art of Teaching,* by Gilford Highet, Alfred A. Knopf, Inc., New York, 1950, page 117, relating the story of Montaigne's response to the question of motivating learners.
2. *Mastering the Teaching of Adults*, by Jerold Apps, Krieger Publishing Co., Melbourne, FL, 1990.
3. *The Morning of the Magicians,* by Louis Pauwels and Jacques Bergier, Scarborough House, Chelsea, MI, 1960, pp 9-15, on the frontiers of knowledge.

Chapter 5. Choosing the Best Setup
1. *Helping Adults Learn and Change,* by Russell D. Robinson, Omni Books, Milwaukee, WI, 1979, page 97.
2. *The Total Immersion Learning Environment,* by Coleman Lee Finkel, National Conference Center, New York, NY, 1987, page 42.

Chapter 6. Moving in Presenter Space
1. *People Space: The Making and Breaking of Human Boundaries,* Norman Ashcroft and Albert E. Scheflen, Anchor Books, Garden City, NY, 1976, pages 68-74.
2. *Tight Spaces: Hard Architecture and How to Humanize It,* by Robert Sommer, Prentice-Hall, Inc., Englewood Cliffs, NJ, 1974, page 94.

Chapter 7. Spicing Up Teaching Tools.
1. *How to Conduct Training Seminars,* by Lawrence S. Munson, McGraw-Hill Book Company, New York, NY, 1984, page 101.
2. *Flip Charts: How to Draw Them and How to Use Them,* by Richard C. Brandt, Brandt Management Group, Richmond, VA, 1986.

Chapter 8. Stirring Imaginations Visually.
1. *Using Charts and Graphs, 1000 Ideas for Visual Persuasion,* by Jan V. White, R.R. Bowker Company, New York, NY, 1984.

Chapter 9. Adding a Touch of High Tech
1. *Presentation Products Magazine,* Full Circle Communications, Malibu, CA.
2. *Technological Horizons in Education* (THE) Journal, Tustin, CA.

Chapter 10. Reacting to Time of Day
1. *Course Trends,* Julie Coates, Editor, Learning Resources Network (LERN), Manhattan, KS.
2. *Seasonality,* by Philip Whatley, Learning Resources Network (LERN), Manhattan, KS, 1990.

Chapter 11. Controlling the Natural Factors
1. Anver Suleiman, *The Marketing Federation,* St. Petersburg Beach, FL.
2. Munson, page 110.
3. *Lighting Handbook, Illuminating Engineering Society,* Illuminating Engineering Society, New York, NY, 1972.

Chapter 12. Planning Tips to Start
1. *How to Teach Adults,* William A. Draves, Learning Resources Network (LERN), Manhattan, KS, 1984.
2. *Tips for Testimonials,* Learning Resources Network (LERN), Manhattan, KS.

Chapter 13. Setting the Mood
1. The Lind Institute, P.O. Box 14487, San Francisco, CA.
2. *Passion for Excellence,* by Tom J. Peters and Nancy K. Austin, Random House, New York, 1985.

Bibliography

1. *People Space: The Making and Breaking of Human Boundaries,* by Norman Ashcraft and Albert E. Scheflen, Anchor Books, Garden City, NY, 1976.

2. *Designing Learning Environments,* Edited by Phillip J. Sleeman and D. M. Rockwell, Longman, Inc., New York, NY, 1981.

3. *Tight Spaces: Hard Architecture and How to Humanize It,* by Robert Sommer, Prentice-Hall, Inc., Englewood Cliffs, NJ, 1974.

4. *The Total Immersion Learning Environment,* by Coleman Lee Finkel, National Conference Center, New York, NY, 1987.

5. *Creating Environments for Effective Adult Learning,* Roger Hiemstra, Editor, Jossey-Bass, Inc., San Francisco, CA 1991.

6. *Helping Adults Learn and Change,* by Russell D. Robinson, Omni Books, Milwaukee, WI, 1979 (First Edition).

7. *How to Create and Market a Successful Seminar or Workshop,* by Howard L. Shenson, Everest House, New York City, NY, 1981.

8. *How to Conduct Training Seminars,* by Lawrence S. Munson, McGraw-Hill Book Company, New York, NY, 1984.

9. *Morning of the Magicians,* by Louis Pauwels and Jacques Bergier, Scarborough House, Chelsea, MI, 1960.

10. *Improving Conference Design and Outcomes,* Paul J. Ilsley, Editor, New Directions for Continuing Education, Number 28, Jossey-Bass Inc., San Francisco, 1985.

About the Author

William A. Draves, CAE, is president of the Learning Resources Network (LERN), an international association in lifelong learning.

A speaker, author, and consultant, he has 25 years experience in adult learning and programming classes and seminars for adults. He has given presentations all over North America, and in the United Kingdom, Germany and Australia.

He holds a master's degree in adult education from The George Washington University in Washington, DC, and obtained Certified Association Executive recognition from the American Society of Association Executives in 1989. He attended Carleton College and graduated from the University of Wisconsin in Madison with honors in 1971.

He is a co-founder of LERN and has been its executive officer since 1976. Prior to his work at LERN, he worked for Kansas State University, University for Man, both in Manhattan, KS; USDA Graduate School in Washington, DC; and Eastside Community Center in Milwaukee.

Draves has written more than 20 publications, including "Pricing Seminars and Conferences," "High Response Surveys," and "Ratios for Success."

His books include "How to Teach Adults," which is now in its eighth printing and second edition, "The Successful Presenter," and "The Free University: A Model for Lifelong Learning." "How to Teach Adults" has been translated into Japanese and Spanish, while "The Successful Presenter" has been translated into Chinese with the title "How to Teach Adults in One Hour."

The Learning Resources Network (LERN)

The Learning Resources Network (LERN) is an international association in lifelong learning, providing information and consulting expertise to any organization offering lifelong learning programming.

Begun in 1974, LERN is a nonprofit tax-exempt educational organization with its headquarters office located in Manhattan, Kansas, USA.

LERN has more than 5,000 members in 12 countries. It provides publications, newsletters, seminars, conferences, consulting, training, technical assistance and membership services to its members and customers all over the world.

LERN serves a variety of organizations involved in lifelong learning programming, including colleges and universities, associations, community colleges, business and private industry, vocational-technical institutes, public schools, hospitals, recreation departments, museums, community groups, social service agencies, churches and independent organizations.

For more information, contact: Learning Resources Network (LERN), 1550 Hayes Drive, Manhattan, KS 66502, USA; Phone: 913-539-5376; Fax: 913-539-7766.

Index

A

B

C